Now 2 Know!

STEM-ing The Tide:

How a STEM Career is Your Life Preserver in the U.S. Economy

by T. G. D'Alberto

 Pithy Professor Publishing Company
Brighton, CO

Published by

Pithy Professor Publishing Company, LLC
PO Box 33824
Northglenn, CO 80233

Copyright © 2015 by
Pithy Professor Publishing Company, LLC

No part of this publication may be reproduced or translated except as permitted under Sections 107 or 108 of the 1976 United States Copyright Act, without the prior written permission of the Publisher.

ISBN: 978-0-9882054-8-2

Library of Congress Control Number: 2015936810

Cover photo: sail boat under the storm, detail on the winch
© il-fede – Fotolia

Printed in the United States of America

About the Author

Dr. Tiffanie G. D'Alberto has a Ph.D. in Electrical & Computer Engineering from Cornell University and a B.S. and M.S. in Electrical Engineering from Virginia Polytechnic Institute & State University. She has worked for over a decade in the telecommunications and aerospace industries as a scientist, project manager, and supervisor.

In her spare time, Tiffanie enjoys oil painting, drawing, reading, sewing, and running. She's a huge fan of Star Trek, Renaissance Festivals, and animals.

Dedication

To Colin

Without whom this book would not be possible

To my grandparents

Without whom I would not be possible

Acknowledgements

I always thank my family first: My parents for the foundation, the push, and the belief in me all along; my fiancé for his inspiration, encouragement, and unending support.

I also want to thank my grandparents in particular. They came to an America on the brink of the Great Depression. Their numerous sacrifices and continuous fights against hardship and prejudice created new hope and new opportunities for generations to come. Their adherence to the best of Old World ethics was a beacon in dark times.

I'd like to thank Amazon.com and CreateSpace for their excellent publish-on-demand service that enables books such as these. And, I thank you, the reader, for making this investment in your future.

Table of Contents

Introduction	1
Chapter 1: The Tide	5
The Disappearing Middle Class	7
The American Dream?	13
Final Thoughts	19
References	20
Chapter 2: The STEM	25
Compensation	27
Stability	30
Impact	33
Other Career Paths	36
The Major STEM Myths & Fears	39
References	42
Chapter 3: Learning Math	45
Math in General	47
Logic	47
Bookkeeping	50

Pattern Seeking	52
Abstraction	54
When Will I Ever Need Math?	56
The NOW 2 kNOW™ Math Series	57
Answers to the Riddles	58

Chapter 4: The Costs of College — **59**

A Breakdown of College Costs	61
Paying for College	63
Making College Pay Off	69
References	71

Chapter 5: Getting Through College — **73**

Undergraduate School - Logistics	75
Undergraduate School - Survival	77
Graduate School - Logistics	81
Graduate School - Survival	85

Chapter 6: Women & STEM — **87**

Statistics	89
Interest	93
Ability	96
Discrimination	100
Other	101
References	102

Chapter 7: Minorities & STEM — 105

    Statistics — 107

    Interest — 110

    Ability — 111

    Discrimination — 117

    Other — 118

    References — 120

Chapter 8: Choose a STEM Career — 123

    Guided Questions — 125

    Impact — 126

    Day to Day Experiences — 129

    Preparation — 132

    Final Comments — 135

Index — 136

Introduction

This book is written for those who are looking for a reliable means to gain financial success in an economy that favors the privileged. Maybe you are in high school pondering your next move. Maybe you've been working for a while and are thinking of making a career change. No matter where you are in life, this book is aimed to help you. Maybe this is your plan B, so to speak, if the sports or acting career doesn't pan out. That's okay. Having a stable, high-paying career option affords many opportunities.

Getting advice from a stranger on such a major life decision requires some leap of faith. So, let me tell you a little about myself so you come to know me better. I have a bit of an unconventional story in that I'm not some perfect student with a laser focus on science that bored straight through 8 years of college, strolling her way into success wondering why so few others were following her lead.

I went to Virginia Tech when I was 17 with the intent to become a veterinarian – I adore animals. In the first two years I learned a few things: 1.) arrogance was not going to get good grades, and I needed to change my approach to college; 2.) memorization was not my thing, and I needed to change majors; and 3.) I am a much stronger person than I realized, and I pushed through significant personal obstacles to get my first degree. I eventually learned how to study and stop freezing on exams, and I changed my major to Electrical Engineering.

I was extremely fortunate that my father paid for my first years in college. After my parents' divorce, we agreed that I should take over my expenses except for $150/month that he gave me toward rent. I will be forever grateful for all of the sacrifices my dad made to invest in my future. Once I was able to take over the majority of my expenses, I took every other semester off to work. Between that and changing majors, it took some time to get through the B.S. degree.

I was able to earn in-state status and eventually landed a cooperative education assignment with the FDA Medical Electronics Branch where I was introduced to fiber optics. I found a fiber optics research group on campus that allowed undergraduates, and I volunteered there for two semesters. It paid off in the end because it paved the way for my M.S. degree. The professor I worked with was willing to be my advisor and even had a research project ready to go. I was thrilled to earn a stipend and remember telling my dad with pride that on $14,400 a year, I wouldn't need help with rent anymore. I finished my M.S. in 1 ½ years, anxious to get on with my life after the delays of the undergraduate degree.

I went to work for a Fortune 500 company in the field of fiber optic component development. I worked there as a scientist, supervisor, and project manager for six years. When the telecom industry crashed, I returned to school for my Ph.D.

I was fortunate enough to find a wonderful advisor at Cornell who worked with my awkward schedule and short time commitment. I had a mortgage in Corning, so I had to commute an hour each way to Ithaca to attend school. Living off my savings, stock options, and a small stipend, I needed to finish in an abbreviated time frame. With much help from my advisor, I was able to meet my goal. It was hard going back to school, and financial issues were regular threats to my ability to continue on, but I made it!

I then landed a research position with a large government contractor working on lasers. I was able to work as a scientist and project manager with some of the most gifted people in the field. I stayed there for five years before taking a sabbatical to write these books and fix up a house in the Caribbean.

I'm not a one-dimensional math/science person (I don't know if I've ever even met one of those). Ok, I do love Star Trek. But, I also love to paint and draw. I sew and have made costumes for the Renaissance Festivals that I try to regularly attend. I "ran" a marathon while getting my Ph.D., and I enjoy snorkeling. I still adore animals, and we adopt as many dogs and cats from the shelters as we can care for. I also like reading fiction and non-fiction alike.

The other thing I love to do is help people learn. I've been tutoring since I can remember: teaching my brother how to read before he got to kindergarten, helping students with math throughout my school career, assisting teachers in remedial courses, instructing undergrads in various classes and work assignments, and training colleagues in industry.

But, that's enough about me. Let's focus on your future. In Chapter 1 we will examine the tide – the forces that threaten to capsize our efforts to gain financial success. In Chapter 2, we talk about how getting a degree in science, technology, engineering, or math (STEM) is a sure fire way to stay afloat in the American economy. In Chapters 3 – 7, we address some of the obstacles involved with STEM studies including a fear of math, paying for college, surviving college, and defying the odds as a woman and/or underrepresented minority. The final chapter is designed to give you tools to find your best career fit.

No matter where the currents of life take you, I wish you great success!

Chapter 1: The Tide

For the first time in our history, the next generation is expected do worse than the prior generation [1]. Yes, I'm talking to you, Millennials. But is that because you are "entitled and lazy"? Or, more likely, are there other issues in play?

Public four year college costs have risen 54% in a time when household income has fallen leaving students with record-breaking debt [1]. As a result of this debt, stagnant minimum wages, and other economic factors, the age income gap is widening: a 30 year old in 2013 had only 79% of the net worth of a 30 year old in 1983 whereas a 60 year old had more than double the net worth across the same time span [1].

The American economy has been turbulent in recent years with the Great Recession and the long recovery. Massive wealth inequality, a non-living minimum wage, loss of manufacturing jobs, and soaring college costs are part of the tide that threatens to overtake us all. Unemployment levels and falling home prices add to the forces that would take us under.

Citizens of Pakistan and Japan enjoy more class mobility than U.S. citizens [2]. Pakistan! Japan! About one third of U.S. children have seen their families' income decline in recent decades [3], and the income inequality problem continues to grow at rapid pace [4].

In this chapter we will examine just how bad things have gotten. We will take an honest look at the gale forces set against us. Hold fast, though, for in Chapter 2 we will discover how to keep the boat from capsizing.

The Disappearing Middle Class

Income and wealth inequality in the U.S. is staggering. The richest are earning more and more and increasing their net worth at alarming rates while the rest of the country falls behind. Figure 1-1 illustrates how from 1980 – 1992, only the top 10% of the country saw their share of income rise whereas the rest of the nation saw just the opposite [5].

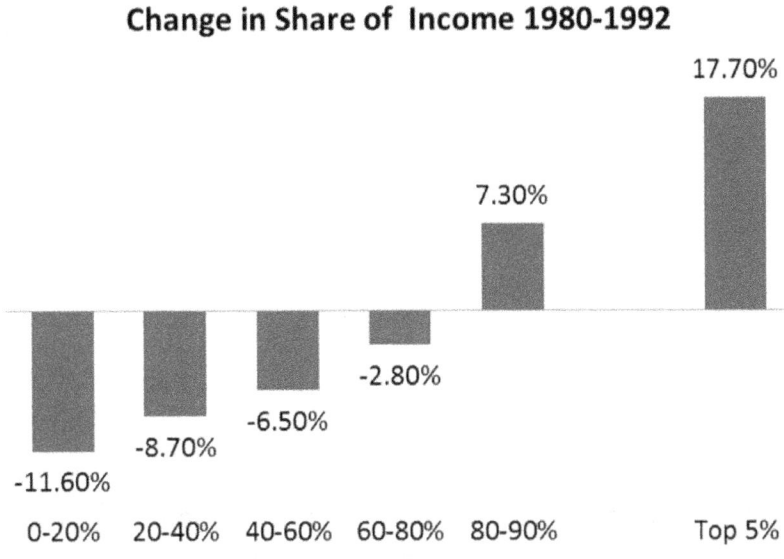

Figure 1-1: Change in income share of wealth classes from 1980 – 1992 [5].

We are looking at this particular period of time because it reflects when the idea of "trickle-down economics" became a popular idea with the legislation to back it. Trickle-down economics preaches that by making the rich richer, the extra money will eventually filter down to the poor via job creation. What are we? Lichen at the bottom of a sewer drain hoping the privileged flush their toilets tonight?

Figure 1-2 shows the result of trickle-down economics in more recent history [6]. Both income and net worth have risen for the wealthy while the rest of the nation has lost even more ground.

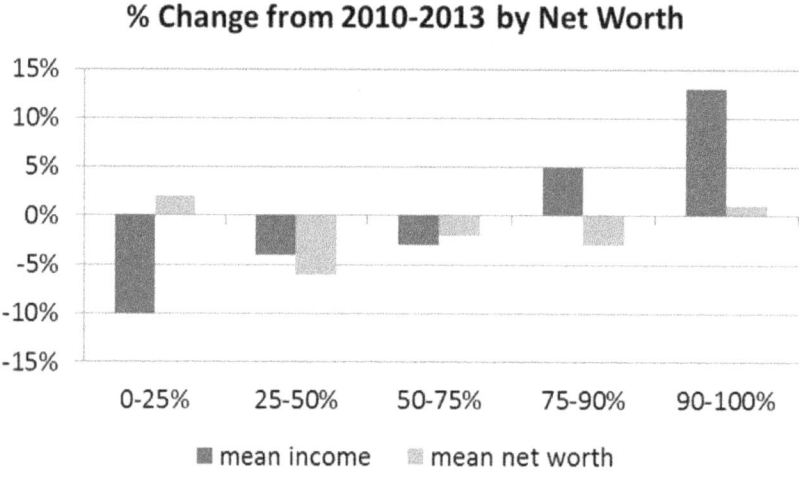

Figure 1-2: Change in income and net worth of wealth classes from 2010 – 2013 [6].

It seems logical to me that if you give a rich man free money, he'll spend it on what he needs and hoard the rest. If you give a poor man free money, he'll spend it on what he needs and hoard the rest. But, there are two key differences: 1.) a few rich guys splitting the money will only have to buy a little whereas a mass of poor men splitting the same amount of money will need to spend most of it to fulfill their needs; 2.) it is when the poor man spends all of this money that the rich are incentivized to create products, services, and the resulting JOBS, to get that money.

These distributions in the changes of income and net worth have produced predictable results. The wealth inequality is worsening. In 1970, the income of the top 1% was 10% of national income levels; in 2012, that percentage more than doubled [4]. In the late seventies, the top 0.1% held 7% of the national wealth; in 2012, that number rose to 22% [4]. In fact, the bottom

90% of people in 2012 own only 22.8% of the wealth, edging out the top 0.1% by only 0.8% [7].

Let me repeat that last statistic: by 2012 the top 0.1% owned about as much wealth as the bottom 90%! Figure 1-3 further illustrates these extremes with the 2010 distribution of net worth and financial wealth (wealth that does not include primary residence ownership)[8]. The distributions only grow more exaggerated with passing years.

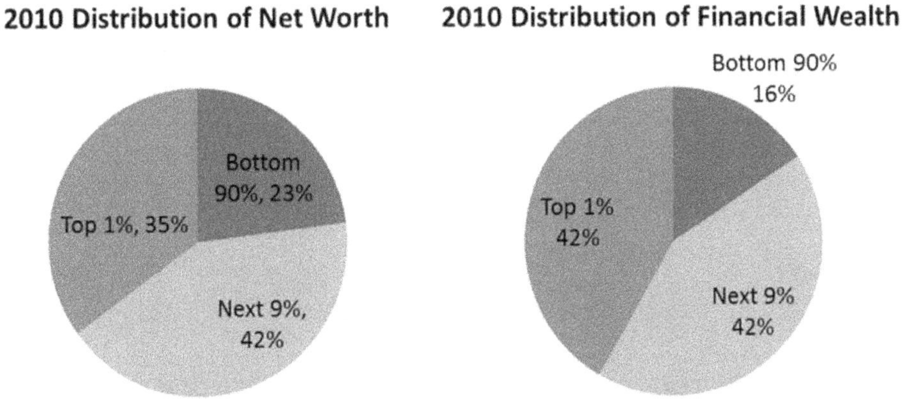

Figure 1-3: Distribution of net worth and non-home wealth in 2010 [8].

Most of us are capitalists to one degree or another, and some imbalance is to be expected. So the question arises, have we reached an *intolerable* level of inequality? One answer to the question lies in the idea of fairness. From 1995 – 2012, worker productivity has risen over 37% but median real wages have only risen <10% [1]. That seems pretty unfair to me. (And though this statistic encompasses many age groups, with so many people retiring and with new talent entering the workforce, it also seems to be another jab at the idea that Millennials are just lazy.)

Another way to answer the question of whether the inequality has become intolerable is to determine whether our standard of living is being negatively impacted. Figure 1-4 gives the average annual consumer price index (CPI) from 1913 – 2014 [9]. To illustrate the meaning of CPI, the chart shows that an item that could be bought for less than $10 in 1913 would have cost $82 in 1980, $172 in 2000, and just under $237 in 2014. Have your wages been keeping pace?

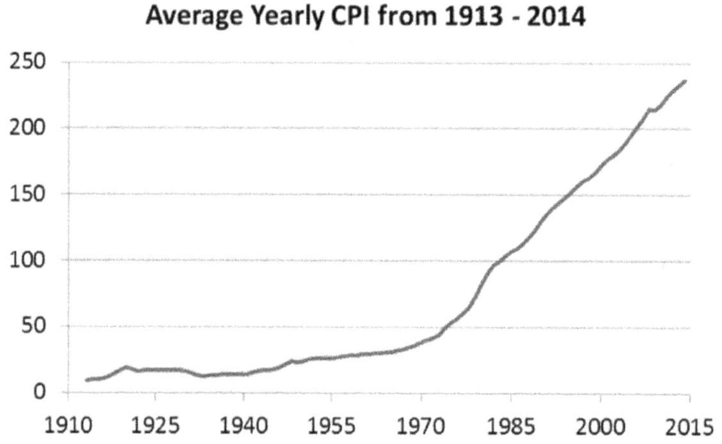

Figure 1-4: The consumer price index (CPI) from 1913 – 2014 [9].

In the time span shown in Figure 1-4, average income increased over 4000%, so some might argue that since the cost of food only went up 400-3800%, depending on the staple, our standard of living has increased [10]. But, averages don't tell the story for the poor and even many of the middle class. In the media today, the wealthiest family in America, the Waltons of Wal-Mart, are constantly under fire for not paying a living wage which the rest of the taxpayers have to subsidize with welfare and food stamps. The typical excuse is that the cost of goods would go up if employees were paid more. How about reducing your extravagant income and reducing my tax load which would allow me to buy more of your products (which I might actually do when I'm not boycotting you over this issue)?

Figure 1-5 shows how the change in CPI from 1978 stacks up against the change in federal minimum wage [9,11]. Clearly those people at the low end of the earnings structure are not able to keep pace. Some states are moving to have local minimum wages that are higher than the federal level (see reference [12] for more detailed information). But, if you are in the tip-based service industry, you know that the decades old $2.13 per hour isn't keeping pace with anyone.

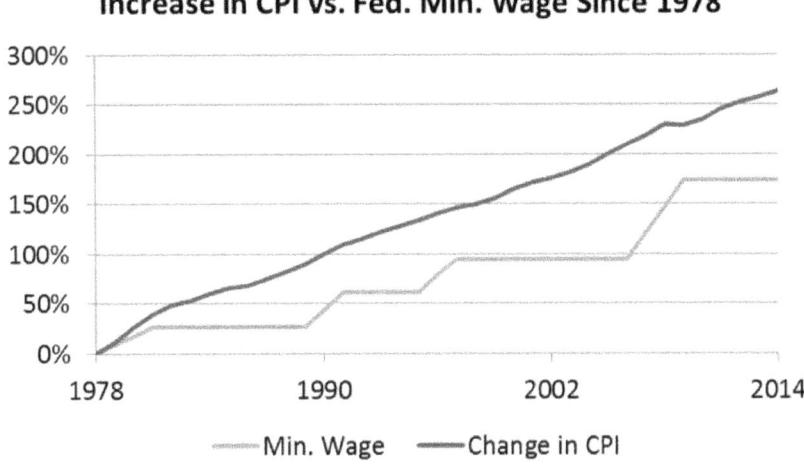

Figure 1-5: Change in CPI vs. federal minimum wage since 1978 [9,11].

Let me add that I personally hate the excuse that most minimum wage jobs are held by teenagers wanting pizza money and therefore we shouldn't be concerned. First of all, the average age of the minimum wage worker is 35 with more than half over the age of 30 [13]. Second, there are many teens, and people in their 20's, who are using minimum wage jobs to help their families make ends meet or to help to pay for college. People deserve to be paid fairly for their work, regardless of their age.

And, speaking of age, if you think that the social security benefit will save you in retirement, if it still exists, you may want to look at Figure 1-6. The cost of living adjustment (COLA) for social security benefits against year to year inflation is not keeping up [9,14].

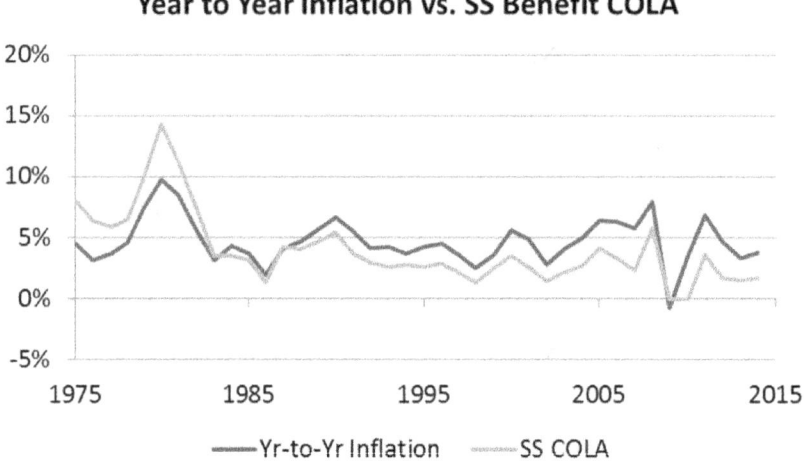

Figure 1-6: Year to year inflation (change in CPI) vs. social security (SS) benefit cost of living adjustment (COLA) [9,14].

The way social security works is that you pay into the system on money you earned under the cap ($117,000 per year in 2014) until you stop working [15]. Your inflation adjusted highest earnings over 35 years is used to calculate your benefit on a graduated basis [15]. For reference, if you turned 66 this year and made about $22,000 in 2014 dollars for 35 years, you would receive just over $13,000 per year in benefits. If you earned the maximum cap amount or more for those 35 years, then you would earn just over $32,000 per year. Some of your benefit may be taxable. Obviously, you will have to make lifestyle adjustments if you plan to survive on social security alone. But, since your cost of living increase on your benefit won't keep up with the actual cost of living, you will be making further lifestyle adjustments on a regular basis.

Finally, in terms of taking care of our health needs, the cost of insurance premiums rose 50% from 2003 – 2010, and employee contributions to health benefits rose 63% in the same period [16]. With the advent of the Affordable Care Act, there has been concern that employers will force workers to <30 hours per week to avoid having to offer benefits. It is unclear at this time if that is the case or if fewer hours are the result of a slow economic recovery [17], but it's sad that we have to wonder how far a corporation would go to avoid paying health benefits to its employees.

Couple health care costs with increased CPI and lower wages, and it is starting to seem that we have indeed reached an intolerable level of inequality.

The American Dream?

The American dream, that which many of us think separates us from all other cultures, is the idea of class mobility. We believe that if we work hard enough we can escape a lower economic class. The trajectory we are on where the rich get richer and the poor get poorer would argue against that belief.

As mentioned in the introduction, places like Pakistan and Japan as well as Canada, France, and Denmark provide more class mobility than the U.S. [2]. The common thread world-wide is that those countries with the highest levels of income or wealth inequality have the lowest class mobility [3].

In 2010, historian Tony Judt wrote [4]:

> *There has been a collapse in intergenerational mobility: in contrast to their parents and grandparents, children today in the UK as in the US have very little expectation of improving upon the condition into which they were born. The poor stay poor. Economic disadvantage for the overwhelming majority translates into ill health, missed educational opportunity, and—increasingly—the familiar symptoms of depression: alcoholism, obesity, gambling, and minor criminality.*

Back in the days of unions and U.S. manufacturing, a middle class could be sustained with jobs that didn't require a college education. Unfortunately, from 1991 – 2012, the U.S. has lost almost one fourth of all factory jobs [18]. And, recent efforts to put government money into rebuilding our infrastructure have almost completely fallen flat. Today, college seems the only ticket to reasonable or high paying jobs. Figure 1-7 shows unemployment rates and median wages for various educational backgrounds in 2013 [19]. On both counts, college education makes a dramatic impact.

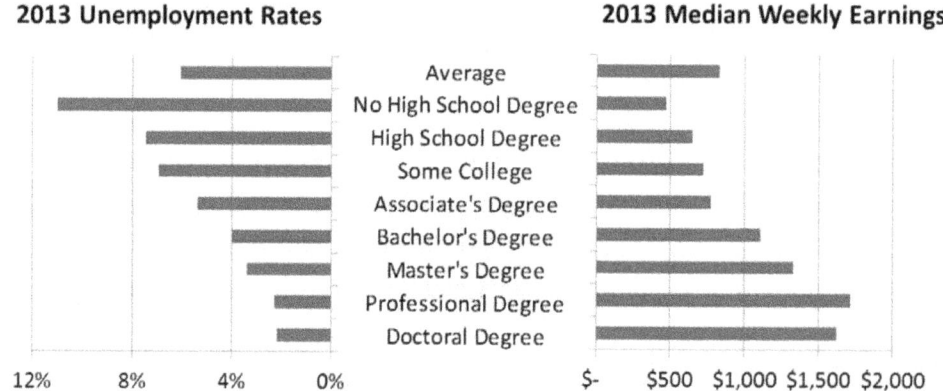

Figure 1-7: 2013 Unemployment rates and median wages by education level [19].

Furthermore, we can track income levels and net worth across varying educational backgrounds during the recovery from the Great Recession, as shown in Figure 1-8 [6]. Once again, those with at least some college are faring much better than their counterparts.

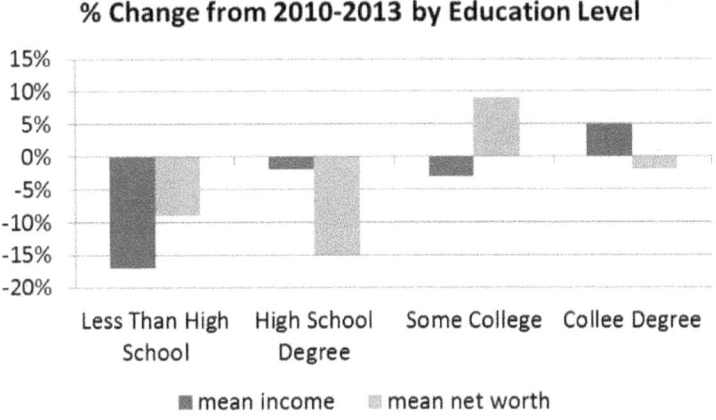

Figure 1-8: Percent change in mean income and mean net worth from 2010 – 2013 by education level [6].

The above figure is working with averages over a three year time span. The people with some college are earning more than those without, so even though their income may have fallen, their net worth continues to rise. For those lucky enough to complete a college degree, their already high income continued to rise. However, because they are high earners, it is likley they bought a home. Home values have taken a hit over recent years which coupled with student debt is having a slight negative impact on their overall net worth. Despite these setbacks, though, clearly those with at any level of college education are doing far better than those without.

We can look at college in terms of return on investment, like any other significant asset. Attending college with the resulting increase in income and net worth seems a good bet. As shown in Figure 1-9, attending any amount of college is ranked as a better investment then even stocks or gold [3].

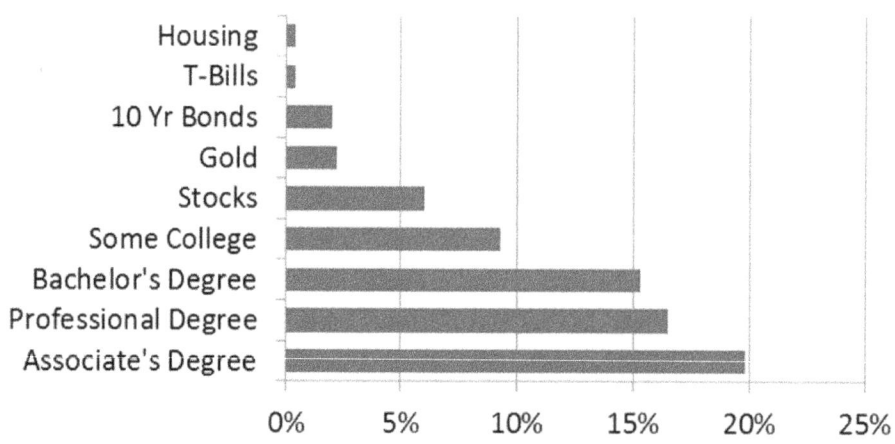

Figure 1-9: Relative return on investment for college compared to other common investment vehicles [3].

That's great, but college is expensive and growing more expensive each year. Figure 1-10 tracks the cost of various colleges both public and private as well as 2- and 4-year institutions from 1981 – 2012 [20]. The federal government does award Pell Grants, free money to attend undergraduate programs, on a financial need basis. Most Pell Grants are only awarded to families below the poverty level (~$20,000 per year income) and the maximum amount is low: only $5,635 for the 2013 – 2014 school year [21]. However, if you do get awarded a Pell Grant, you may also qualify for other need-based aid [21].

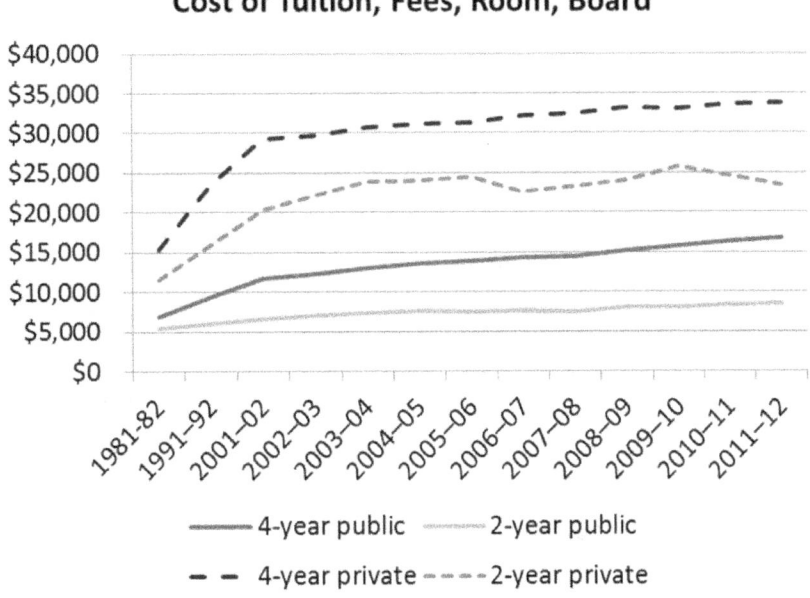

Figure 1-10: Costs of college from 1981 – 2012 [20].

So, college seems like a no-brainer for the very rich and perhaps maybe almost an achievable struggle for the very poor. But as Figure 1-11 points out, the very small amount of aid that is available to the poor, coupled with other factors we'll discuss in Chapter 7, make college degree attainment disproportionately more likely for the rich [22]. Between 1970 and 2013, enrollment and graduation rates both increased for students of families in the top 25% and the bottom 25%; however, the top quartile currently graduates at a rate almost four times that of the lower quartile [22]. And, there is still a large section of middle income earners with even fewer options.

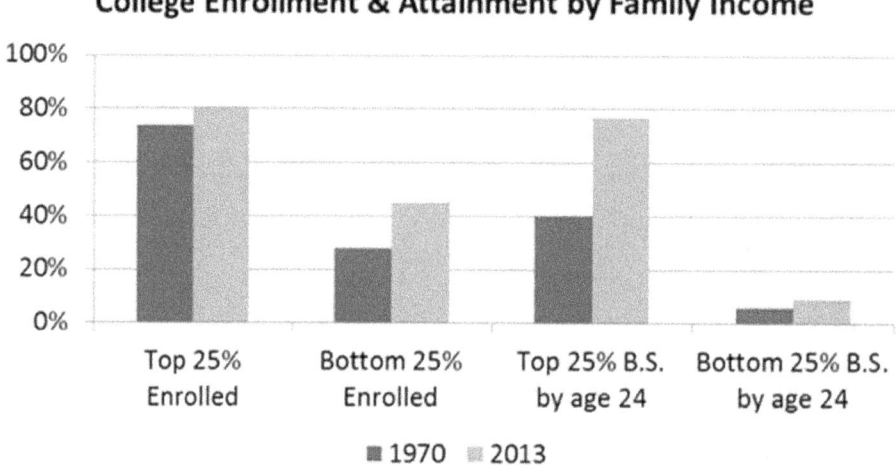

Figure 1-11: College enrollment & B.S. attainment by family income [22].

As a final note in this section, an important underlying assumption of the American dream is social equality, that we can enjoy class mobility no matter gender, race, or background. Unfortunately, this tenet seems lost, as well. As we'll see in Chapters 6 and 7, women and minorities face an uphill battle. There are far more blacks and Hispanics than whites and Asians attending high poverty schools that ill prepare their students for college success [23]. Since 1970, the achievement gap between low and high income students has increased almost 40% [3].

It would appear that the one ticket to class mobility, the college degree, is not equally accessible to all.

Final Thoughts

Enough with the bad news. There is a way out from under the sinking masses: the answer is still to go to college. The rich have investments and assets. A college education is an investment and an asset, and once you have it, it can't be stolen. But, since college is so expensive, you'll want to make sure your investment will pay off. You'll have to get the *right* degree. You want to graduate with skills that are in demand and well-paid, otherwise you might as well throw your money away. The rest of this book will show you what you need to do and how to overcome the hurdles before you.

To that end, it might be worth looking a little more closely at the 1% we hate on so much. Figure 1-12 shows the occupations of almost 75% of the top 1% [24]. This should give us some clues as to where to go from here.

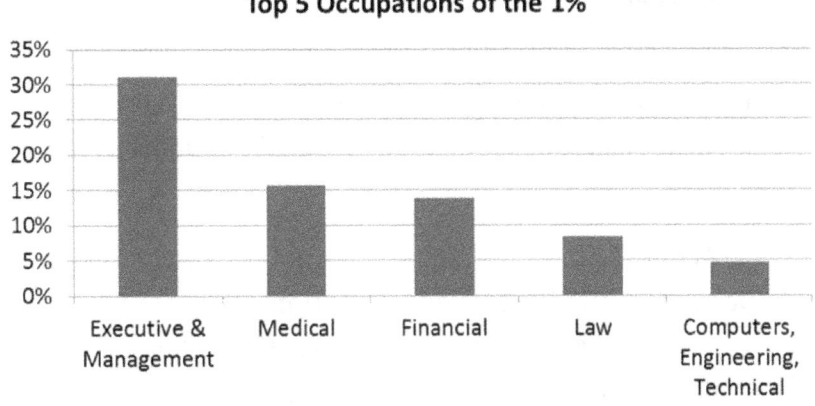

Figure 1-12: Top five occupations of the top 1% [24].

References

[1]   Roos, Dave. "Are Millennials Really the First Generation to do Worse Than Their Parents?" *HowStuffWorks.com*. October 11, 2013: http://money.howstuffworks.com/personal-finance/financial-planning/millennials-first-worse-parents1.htm.

[2]   Hargreaves, Steve. "The Myth of the American Dream," *CNN Money*. New York, December 18, 2013: http://money.cnn.com/2013/12/09/news/economy/america-economic-mobility/.

[3]   Greenstone, Michael *et.al*. "Thirteen Economic Facts About Social Mobility and the Role of Education," *Brookings.edu*. The Hamilton Project, June 2013: http://www.brookings.edu/research/reports/2013/06/13-facts-higher-education.

[4]   Matthews, Chris. "Wealth Inequality in America: It's Worse Than You Think," *Fortune*. Time Inc. Network, October 31, 2014: http://fortune.com/2014/10/31/inequality-wealth-income-us/.

[5]   Jones, Arthur F., Jr and Weinberg, Daniel H. "the Changing Shape of the Nation's Icome Distribution: 1947 – 1998," *Consumer Income*. U.S. Census Bureau, U.S. Department of Commerce, P60-204, June 2000: http://www.census.gov/prod/2000pubs/p60-204.pdf.

[6]   Bricker, Jesse *et. al.* "Changes in U.S. Family Finances from 2010 to 2013: Evidence from the Survey of Consumer Finances," *Federal Reserve Bulletin.* Board of Governers of the Federal Reserve System, Vol. 100, No. 4, September 2014: http://www.federalreserve.gov/pubs/bulletin/2014/pdf/scf14.pdf.

[7]   Saez, Emmanuel and Zucman, Gabriel. "Wealth Inequality in the United States Since 1913: Evidence From Capitalized Income Tax Data," *NBER Working Paper Series.* National Bureau of Economic Research, Working Paper 20625, October 2014: http://gabriel-zucman.eu/files/SaezZucman2014.pdf.

[8]   Domhoff, William G. "Wealth, Income, and Power," *Who Rules America?* Sociology Department, University of California, Santa Cruz, updated February 2013: http://www2.ucsc.edu/whorulesamerica/power/wealth.html.

[9]   McMahon, Tim. "Historical Consumer Price Index (CPI-U) Data," *InflationData.com.* January 16, 2015: http://inflationdata.com/inflation/consumer_price_index/historicalcpi.aspx?reloaded=true.

[10] McMahon, Tim. "Food Price Inflation Since 1913," *InflationData.com.* March 21, 2013: http://inflationdata.com/articles/2013/03/21/food-price-inflation-1913/.

[11] U.S. Department of Labor. "History of Federal Minimum Wage Rates Under the Fair Labor Standards Act, 1938 – 2009," *Wage and Hour Division (WHD).* U.S. Department of Labor: http://www.dol.gov/whd/minwage/chart.htm.

[12] U.S. Department of Labor. "Minimum Wages Laws in the States – January 1, 2015," *Wage and Hour Division (WHD)*. U.S. Department of Labor: http://www.dol.gov/whd/minwage/america.htm.

[13] Bernstein, Jared. "Minimum Wage: Who Makes It?," *The Upshot*. The New York Times, June 9, 2014: http://www.nytimes.com/2014/06/10/upshot/minimum-wage.html?_r=0&abt=0002&abg=1.

[14] Social Security Administration. "Cost of Living Adjustments," *Social Security: Official Social Security Website*: http://www.ssa.gov/oact/cola/colaseries.html.

[15] Social Security Administration. "Your Retirement Benefit: How It's Figured," *www.socialsecurity.gov*. SSA Publication No. 05-10070: http://www.ssa.gov/pubs/EN-05-10070.pdf.

[16] Quinton, Sophie. "Health Premiums Up 50 Percent from 2003 to 2010 – Report," *National Journal*. November 17, 2011: http://www.nationaljournal.com/healthcare/health-premiums-up-50-percent-from-2003-to-2010-report-20111117.

[17] Perkins, Olivera. "Obamacare Not Forcing Workers Into Part-Time Employment, Analyses Find," *Cleveland.com*. September 16, 2014: http://www.cleveland.com/business/index.ssf/2014/09/obamacare_not_forcing_workers.html.

[18] Levinson, Marc. "Measuring the Loss of Manufacturing Jobs," *CRS Insights*. IN10109, July 21, 2014: http://www.fas.org/sgp/crs/misc/IN10109.pdf.

[19] U.S. Bureau of Labor Statistics. "Earnings and Unemployment Rates by Educational Attainment," *Employment Projections*. U.S. Department of Labor, March 24, 2014: http://www.bls.gov/emp/ep_chart_001.htm.

[20] National Center for Education Statistics. "Tuition Costs of Colleges and Universities," *Fast Facts*. IES Institute of Educational Sciences, U.S. Department of Education: http://nces.ed.gov/FastFacts/display.asp?id=76.

[21] Scholarships.com. "Federal Pell Grants," *www.Scholarships.com*: https://www.scholarships.com/financial-aid/federal-aid/federal-pell-grants/.

[22] Korn, Melissa. "Big Gap in College Graduation Rates for Rich and Poor, Study Finds," *The Wall Street Journal*. February 4, 2015: http://finance.yahoo.com/news/big-gap-college-graduation-rates-005300210.html.

[23] U.S. Department of Education. *Higher Education: Gaps in Access and Persistence Study*. Institute of Educational Sciences & National Center for Education Statistics, NCES 2012-046, August 2012: http://nces.ed.gov/pubs2012/2012046.pdf.

[24] Gilson, Dave and Perot, Carolyn. "It's the Inequality, Stupid," *Plutocracy Now*. Mother Jones, March/April 2011 Issue: http://www.motherjones.com/politics/2011/02/income-inequality-in-america-chart-graph.

Chapter 2: The STEM

In old nautical terminology, the stem refers to the mast. The phrase "stem the tide" means steering the mast toward the storm surge to keep the ship afloat. This book is about how to stem the tide of income inequality and class stagnation. In our case, the STEM refers to Science, Technology, Engineering, and Math careers.

The last graphic of Chapter 1 shows that over one third of the top 1% are in medical, financial, computer, engineering, or technical fields, i.e. STEM fields. Another third is in management which can also come from a basis in STEM studies. We now know that a college degree is the ticket to class mobility. In this chapter, we'll see how STEM majors are our best bet. And, with each one of us that makes it, our whole country becomes stronger:

> *President's Council of Advisors on Science and Technology (PCAST 2012) urged colleges and universities at all levels to produce more STEM graduates, announcing that if the United States is to retain its preeminence in science and technology and remain competitive in a fast-changing economy, it will need 1 million more STEM professionals over the next decade than it is currently projected to produce. [1]*

We'll first consider how STEM careers stack up against three of the major factors in choosing a profession: compensation, stability, and impact. We'll then look briefly at careers outside of STEM and then introduce the topic of STEM myths and fears that are addressed in subsequent chapters.

Compensation

STEM careers pay well, and many of the high paying fields require only a four year degree (and some even less!). In 2013-14, PayScale did a survey of over 1000 colleges with graduates holding no higher than the Bachelor's Degree. Figure 2-1 gives the top 10 results of the PayScale survey for graduates with 2 years (initial) and 15 years (mid-career) experience [2]. The common theme – they are all STEM careers. STEM careers also occupy 80% of the next 10 highest mid-career salaries with a four year degree [2].

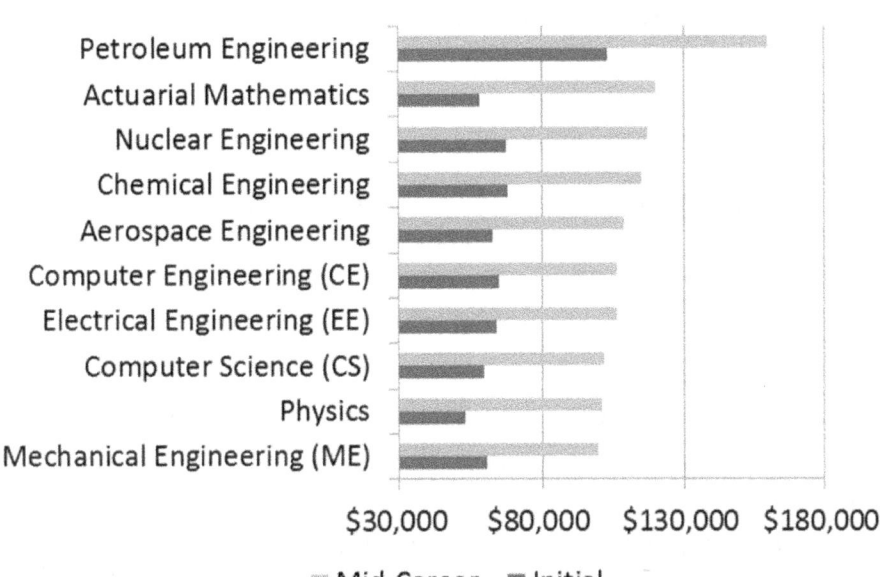

Figure 2-1: Top 10 median salaries by 4-yr degree [2].

We can also lift the educational requirement and examine salaries across all job descriptions. Figure 2-2 shows the top 10 highest mean salaries for non-management positions as published by the Bureau of Labor Statistics [3]. Mean salaries are averaged across all educational and experience levels. Notice that STEM careers occupy 90% of this list.

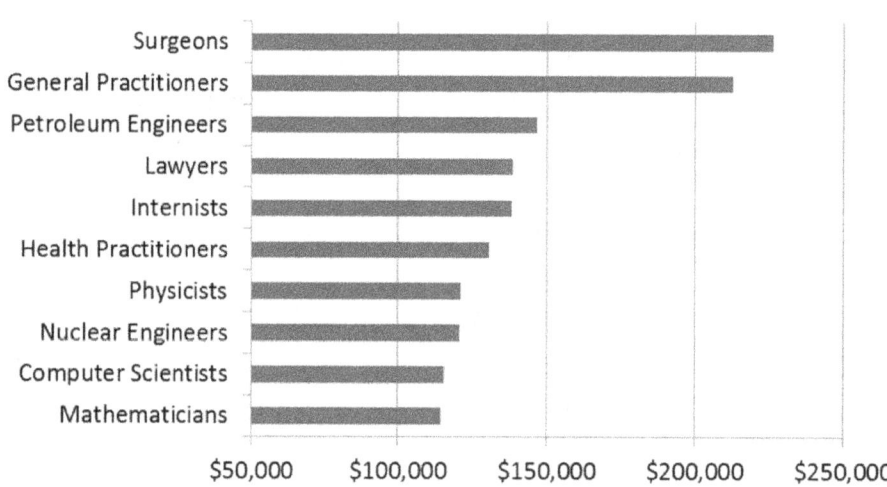

Figure 2-2: Top 10 2013 overall mean salaries for non-managers [3].

But, compensation includes many factors in addition to salary. With any professional job comes many perks. Bonus pay is quite common for meeting goals or even as a yearly installment (the infamous Christmas bonus, for example). Stock options can also be part of a bonus structure or built into your pay. Stock options are company stocks that you can cash out for the profit amount if the price of the stock goes up in a specified period of time.

Benefits are a subset of compensation, and they encompass many things. In terms of financial perks, most companies will offer a retirement plan, often called a 401k. In such plans, you can opt to contribute a portion of your pay to invest in stocks or funds, and the company usually matches some percentage of that contribution on your behalf. Some companies also fund programs similar to pension plans. No more worrying about social security keeping up with inflation!

Benefits also include health benefits. Companies typically pick up a large share of medical, dental, and vision insurance plans for the employee and his or her dependents. Life insurance is also usually offered at a significant discount. Safeguards against short- and long-term disability may also be offered to offset income loss in case of a disaster.

Benefits also include paid time off flexibility like vacation and sick leave. Many companies have unlimited sick leave as long as you don't abuse it. Still other companies are experimenting with unlimited vacation time, as well.

Other benefits in professional jobs include travel opportunities (for business purposes) with reasonable meal and transportation costs paid for you. Some companies work out various kinds of consumer discounts for their employees. Also, many people find that the company will work with them to fund additional degrees if it helps them in their job.

Special benefits are also included for certain professionals, especially those with advanced degrees. For instance, relocation assistance is wonderful if you have to pick up your life to move to a job location. After my Ph.D. program in New York, I accepted a job in Colorado. The entire move, including packing, shipping, and unpacking of household goods and vehicles, as well as my travel costs were paid in full. In addition, the company paid real estate agent fees and bought a point for my new mortgage. The higher the education and the more in-demand the professional, the more companies are willing to do to recruit and keep you.

Stability

Let me preface this section by stating that recessions, corporate greed, and lay-offs are a fact of life in many, if not all, professions. Your best hedge against the odds is to be in demand. Qualified people in STEM careers are very much sought after. The U.S. Department of Commerce projects that job growth in STEM fields will increase almost double that of non-STEM fields (17% growth versus 10%) [1]. Figure 2-3 shows how very few people are rising to this opportunity. Just under one quarter of B.S. degrees in 2008 were awarded in a STEM field [4]. Only 16% were given in the fields of computer and information science, engineering, physical science, and math [4].

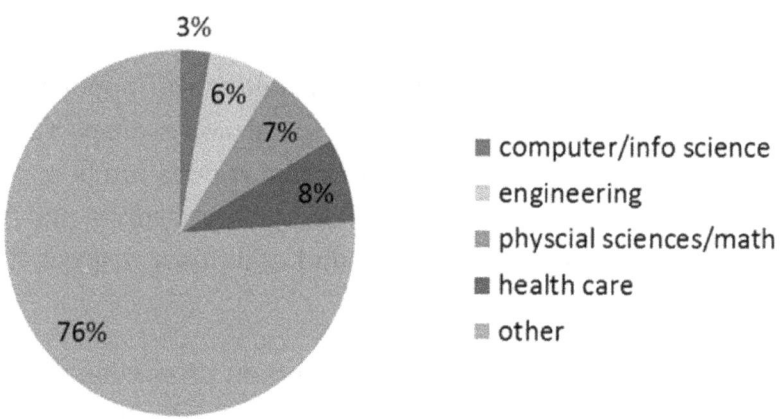

Figure 2-3: 2008 B.S. Degrees [4].

Figure 2-4 shows the outcome of STEM demand in terms of 2012 unemployment numbers [5]. STEM employees (some representative ones are given in the figure) typically fare much better at finding work in comparison to the arts, business, and some law professions.

2012 Unemployment Rate by Occupation

Occupation	Rate
Overall	~7.5%
Physicians & Surgeons	~0.8%
Registered Nurses	~2.5%
Environmental Scientists	~2.5%
Astronomers & Physicists	~0.2%
Computer Scientists	~3.5%
Petroleum Engineers	~0.5%
Electrical Engineers	~3.4%
Aerospace Engineers	~3.8%
Financial Analysts	~2.3%
Accountants & Auditors	~4.2%
Athletes & Related	~8.7%
Writers & Authors	~6.0%
Dancers & Related	~10%
Artists & Related	~6.3%
Loan Counselors & Officers	~7.3%
Admin. Service Managers	~5.3%
Buyers	~4.9%
Paralegals & Legal Assts.	~5.1%
Lawyers	~1.5%

Figure 2-4: 2012 Unemployment rate by occupation (actors & related were unemployed at a rate of >28%) [5].

Again, lay-offs are a part of the corporate world. I've worked for two companies where layoffs happened in droves because of an industry crash or the Great Recession. The difference for the in-demand professional is that future work is easier to come by, and with signing bonuses and relocation assistance, you are not stuck looking for a job in the same town that thousands of others are suddenly looking in. Plus, enjoying a higher salary in the first place means you also have the opportunity to build up your savings to safeguard against sudden lay-offs.

There is a fair question that is usually asked – if everyone gets a STEM degree wouldn't STEM unemployment go up and wages go down? Here's my answer:

1. STEM degrees are challenging, so not everyone can just "get" one.
2. Our reality is becoming more and more technology-based with many areas of the world wanting to catch up, i.e. the demand for STEM people continues to rise.
3. An ever-growing world population translates into an ever-increasing need for innovation in health care and creature comforts.
4. With a true deficit in the number of people who can fulfill these jobs now, demand is apt to be high for a long, long time.
5. IF there is ever a glut of qualified STEM job seekers, it would be decades off when you will then have years of experience over new candidates.
6. The biggest threat perhaps is in other countries that do recognize the need for more STEM people. These countries are actively educating their youth, sometimes with free tuition. However, our universities are widely recognized as premier institutions of study, so degrees earned in the U.S. will still carry a lot of weight.

Impact

With all of that said, what good is a high-paying, stable job if you don't find meaning in it? The good news is that STEM careers have a very large impact in the world we live in. The most obvious examples are in the health sciences or medical fields. Caring for the sick or disabled has direct impact on the quality of a person's life. One on one contact provides immediate feedback to the good work you do. Some careers in this field are just as impactful, but take place in the laboratory rather than in a clinical setting. Curing disease, helping people walk, and saving lives are all worthwhile, impactful occupations. Figure 2.5 gives some examples of jobs in the health sciences field.

Figure 2-5: Examples of health sciences careers.

Also under the general heading of science are the natural and physical sciences. People in these fields help protect the environment and wild animals, keep the world food supply healthy, and predict weather disasters. They also develop new materials like plastics and textiles that enable myriad things from biocompatible medical devices to the flexible glass used in our phones. They investigate the world we live in and strive to help us understand our universe. Figure 2-6 gives some examples of natural science professions.

Natural Sciences	Agricultural & Food Scientist Atmospheric Scientist Biophysicist or Biochemist Chemist or Materials Scientist Environmental Scientist Geoscientist or Hydrologist Marine Biologist or Limnologist Occupational Health & Safety Specialist Physicist or Astronomer Zoologist or Wildlife Specialist

Figure 2-6: Examples of natural sciences careers.

Technology fields are all about computers. Whether it's building a website or making a network run smoothly, many technology careers ensure that businesses can operate effectively. Creating new communications tools and enabling medical models and devices are other areas of impact. Coming up with the new social media site, coding for the next android evolution, or making new and faster machines that might one day hold human consciousness are just a sampling of the many ideas being explored. Figure 2-7 gives some example professions in the technology field.

Technology	Computer & Information Research Scientist Computer & Information Systems Manager Computer Hardware Engineer Computer Programmer Computer Software Engineer/Developer Computer Systems Analyst Database Administrator Network & Systems Administrator Security Analyst or Network Architect Web Developer

Figure 2-7: Examples of technology careers.

Engineering is the broadest category where not even the sky is the limit. Exploring space, designing bridges, and finding energy resources are just a few of the tasks entrusted to engineers. If it's mechanical or electrical, involves new materials, new devices, and new technologies, then the engineer has touched it. It would be impossible to list all of the things engineers do. Figure 2-8 lists some of the engineering occupations.

Enineering	Aerospace Engineer
	Biomedical Engineer
	Chemical Engineer
	Civil Engineer
	Electrical Engineer
	Engineering Technician
	Industrial Engineer
	Marine Engineer or Naval Architect
	Mechanical Engineer
	Mining, Nuclear, or Petroleum Engineer

Figure 2-8: Examples of engineering careers.

In the field of mathematics, you can choose to work on a theoretical basis developing the mathematical tools we require to understand our universe and develop new technologies. Or, you can work directly with individuals and businesses to achieve financial success. Helping someone prepare for retirement, analyzing a market for new goods or services, and ensuring legal and efficient business operations are examples of work in this field. Statistical analysis can be applied to myriad fields including business, medical, sociological, and environmental. Figure 2-9 lists some of the opportunities available in the math domain.

Math	Accountant or Auditor Actuary Economist Cost Estimator Financial Analyst Market Research Analyst Mathemetician Personal Financial Advisor Purchasing Manager Statistician

Figure 2-9: Examples of mathematics careers.

Other Career Paths

STEM careers do not provide the only means of having impactful, rewarding work. There are many worthwhile careers to consider, and if you have a very strong calling to one, you should at least learn more about it. Make sure you understand if the expected salary compensates you for your college expenses, if the hours and stress levels of the occupation are a good fit, and if the projected growth in that field can sustain future employment opportunities. In this section, we'll take a brief look at some of the other careers outside of STEM.

Median salaries for four year graduates of some of the more popular majors are shown in Figure 2-10 [2]. The information used to generate the chart was from the same source as Figure 2-1 (for STEM careers) and is laid out with the same scales for easy comparison. For many of these fields, an advanced degree, perhaps to the Ph.D. level, is required for decent prospects.

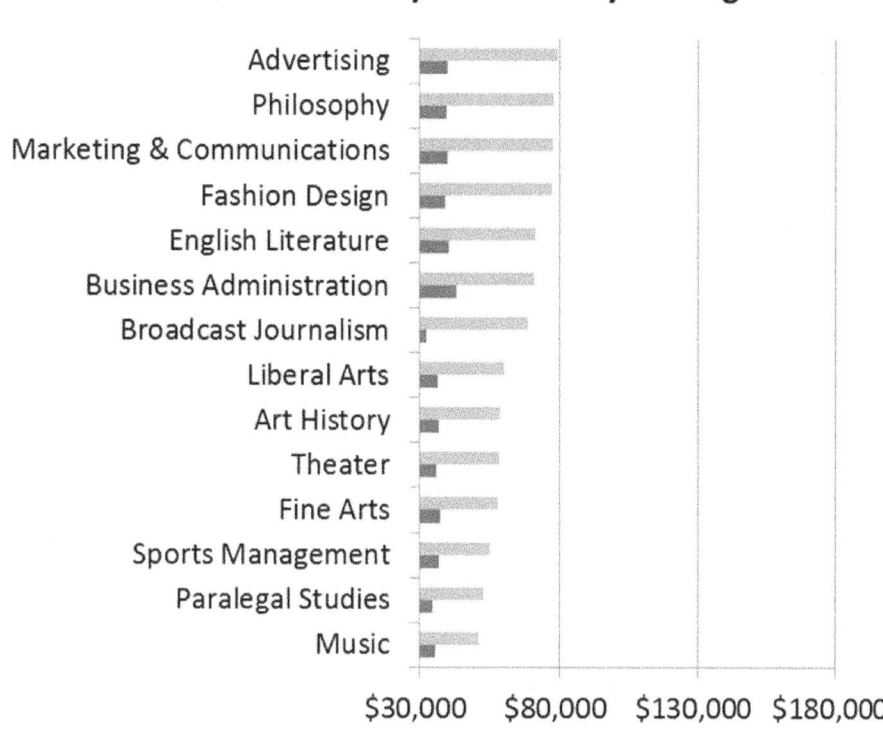

Figure 2-10: Median salaries by selected 4-yr degree [2].

Figure 2.10 is indicative of the kinds of pay many students can expect upon graduating from a four year program. With college costs what they are, it is difficult to justify some of these salaries against the debt that is incurred. The requirement for advanced degrees just adds to that debt. Many STEM fields offer the option of going to graduate school for free or even with a paid part-time job. In other fields, the cost of graduate school is on the student. And, as Figure 2-4 indicates, job stability isn't that great outside of STEM.

For those that can afford to go at least two years beyond the baccalaureate, business and law are popular fields. Figure 2-11 shows the mean salaries of lawyers, some business professionals, and some STEM specialists [3]. It can be readily seed that lawyers make some really good money. And, the unemployment rate for lawyers is extremely low. The Bureau of Labor Statistics predicts a 10% job growth for lawyers, at least as fast as that for all occupations [6].

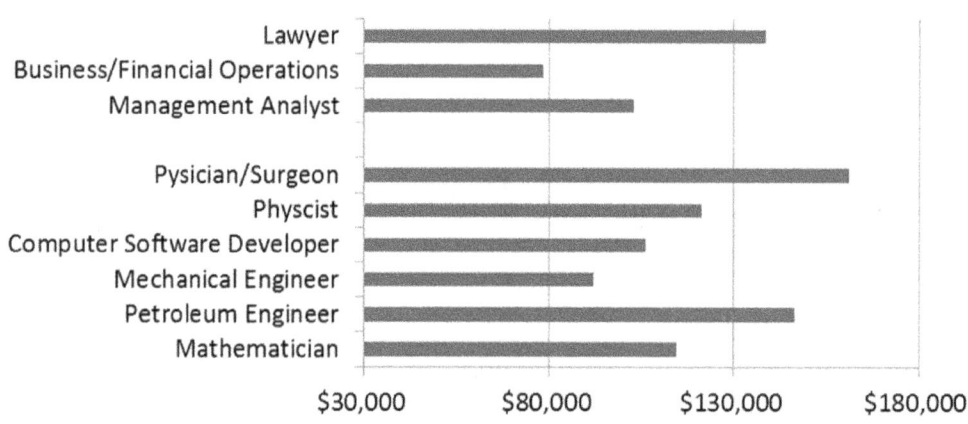

Figure 2-11: 2013 Mean salaries by selected occupation [3].

Unfortunately, mean salaries and unemployment do not tell the whole story when it comes to an occupation. The Bureau also notes that competition for jobs among lawyers is expected to be very high due to more and more qualified graduates in the field [6]. But, far more concerning is the level of dissatisfaction in the field of law. Many lawyers work 80-100 hours per week for years on end in the hopes of making partner. A survey by CareerBliss.com ranked associate advocate as the unhappiest job in America [7] – lawyers actually beat out retail! And, the American Bar Association reports that almost half of all lawyers are unhappy in their jobs; only 40% would recommend the job to others [8]. So, the bottom line is that you should probably really love law if you want to pursue a career in that field.

As for business, it is true that managers and CEO's make more money than their underlings. But, there are many ways to get into the business and management side of industry if that is what interests you. The math fields provide numerous direct avenues, and any STEM field has opportunities for you to move into management, start your own practice, or even head your own corporation. In *Fortune Magazine's* 2014 list of the top 10 most powerful women, only one did not have a STEM degree [9]. In addition, many employers will pay their STEM employees to go back to school for a Master's of Business Administration (M.B.A.). Getting into management requires experience, and getting a four year business degree with no other credentials to back it up may make things pretty hard at first.

As a final comment, I know that some people are very passionate about the arts, design, literature, music, or sports. If you have a very special talent and you know people in the industry that can give you a leg up, go for it! If not, you may really want to look into the costs associated with college versus realistic earnings. Keep in mind that it is possible to minor in these fields, or even have a double major, so that you can keep multiple options open. It's something to consider, anyway.

The Major STEM Myths & Fears

The next five chapters deal in depth with the major misconceptions and fears about STEM careers. The first stumbling block that many students face when considering a career in STEM is math. I've seen students so terrified of math that they convince themselves they just can't do it. I've tutored such students, and I can't count how many times I've heard, "That's all there is to it?" Indeed.

I went into mathematical fields because I found the subject far easier than history with all of its memorization requirements. The fact is, to succeed at math, you need to stop memorizing and start understanding math. Chapter 3 outlines the skills you will need and offers suggestions on honing those skills – without having to do any math!

The second myth about STEM careers is that college is a waste of money. As we've discussed, skipping college or a trade school altogether can greatly reduce your income and quality of life. It is true that the costs of college outweigh the benefits if you choose the wrong major or don't go far enough. For example, there is nothing wrong with majoring in English, but be aware that to make such a major pay off, you very likely will have to pursue graduate studies.

College is a vocational school that should train you for a job. If your school of choice is too expensive or if your major isn't going to pay enough to balance your debt, you may need to reconsider your choices. Many STEM majors offer high paying jobs with only 2 – 4 years of study, and in most non-medical STEM majors, you can go to graduate school for free. Chapter 4 walks you through choosing, planning, and paying for college.

The third fear is that the coursework is too hard. Okay, that one has some validity. Undergraduate programs especially will tax you unlike anything you've experienced to date. Unfortunately, our high schools do not generally prepare us for the autonomy and huge workloads that higher education will demand. In college there is no one to make sure you do your work, no one will care if you fail, and no one wants to hear how overburdened you are. It sounds harsh, but the real world is even worse. There are strategies to get through it, though, and Chapter 5 will help.

The fourth myth that many students buy into is that STEM careers are only for nerdy white males. UNTRUE! Women and minorities can succeed in STEM just as well as white men. There is a horrible underrepresentation of women and minorities in many of these fields, though. We'll talk about why that is and why it shouldn't be so in Chapters 6 & 7. This is a matter of social equality, and women and minorities deserve access to the high paying, stable, and rewarding opportunities of STEM careers.

Finally, as far as envisioning the one-dimensional STEM geek, almost everyone I've met in my career, of either sex and of various ethnicities, enjoys myriad interests outside of STEM. They pursue athletic hobbies such as running, yoga, bike racing, rock climbing, spelunking, and diving to artistic hobbies such as drawing, painting, playing instruments, acting, and writing to other fun endeavors such as building and racing cars, micro-brewing, and traveling the world. And, since they make good money and have flex time, they don't just dabble but actively pursue their interests.

So, let's get over these fears and start to create a wonderful future!

References

[1] U.S. Department of Education. *STEM Attrition: College Students' Paths Into and Out of STEM Fields.* Institute of Educational Sciences & National Center for Education Statistics, NCES 2014-001, November 2013: http://nces.ed.gov/pubs2014/2014001rev.pdf.

[2] PayScale. "2013-2014 College Payscale Salary Report: Majors that Pay You Back," PayScale.com: http://www.payscale.com/college-salary-report-2014/majors-that-pay-you-back.

[3] U.S. Bureau of Labor Statistics. "May 2013 National Industry-Specific Occupational Employment and Wage Estimates: Sector 54 - Professional, Scientific, and Technical Services," *Occupational Employment Statistics.* U.S. Department of Labor, May 2013: http://www.bls.gov/oes/current/naics2_54.htm#13-0000.

[4] U.S. Department of Education. *Today's Baccalaureate: The Fields and Courses that 2007-08 Bachelor's Degree Recipients Studied.* National Center for Education Statistics, NCES 2013-755, May 2013: http://nces.ed.gov/pubs2013/2013755.pdf.

[5] "2012 Jobs Snapshot: Unemployment Rates by Occupation," *The Wall Street Journal.* January 8, 2013: http://www.wsj.com/articles/SB10001424127887323936804578229873392511426.

[6] U.S. Bureau of Labor Statistics. "Lawyers," *Occupational Outlook Handbook 2014-15 Edition.* U.S. Department of Labor, January 8 2014: http://www.bls.gov/ooh/legal/lawyers.htm.

[7]   Smith, Jacquelyn. "The Happiest and Unhappiest Jobs in America," *Forbes*.   March 22, 2013: http://www.forbes.com/sites/jacquelynsmith/2013/03/22/the-happiest-and-unhappiest-jobs-in-america/.

[8]   Kane, Sally. "Legal Career Satisfaction," *About Careers*. 2008: http://legalcareers.about.com/b/2008/02/10/legal-career-satisfaction.htm.

[9]   Gallagher, Leigh. "The Women Who STEM-ed Their Way to Power," *Fortune*. September 22, 2014: http://fortune.com/2014/09/22/women-and-stem/.

Chapter 3: Learning Math

The biggest hurdle to getting into STEM for a lot of people is learning math. I have heard so many students say, "I can't do math," "math is hard," or my favorite, "I'm just not a math person." To this, I have two things to say:

1. Never let any subject, any person, or any thing stand in your way to your future. Get help from the instructor, fellow students, books, or the internet.
2. There are many STEM fields that do not require a lot of math in coursework or in actual practice.

That being said, I will now wax poetic for a second on math. In addition to being a gateway to many high paying jobs, math is the universal language. We use it across cultures to communicate scientific knowledge, and we even send mathematical messages into space to attempt extraterrestrial communication. Math influences our philosophies and religions, helps us understand and explain how the universe works, and enables us to develop tools that prolong our lives or make us more comfortable. It is a way of thinking that when mastered provides the logic and abstraction necessary to ponder concepts that would otherwise be impossible to fathom.

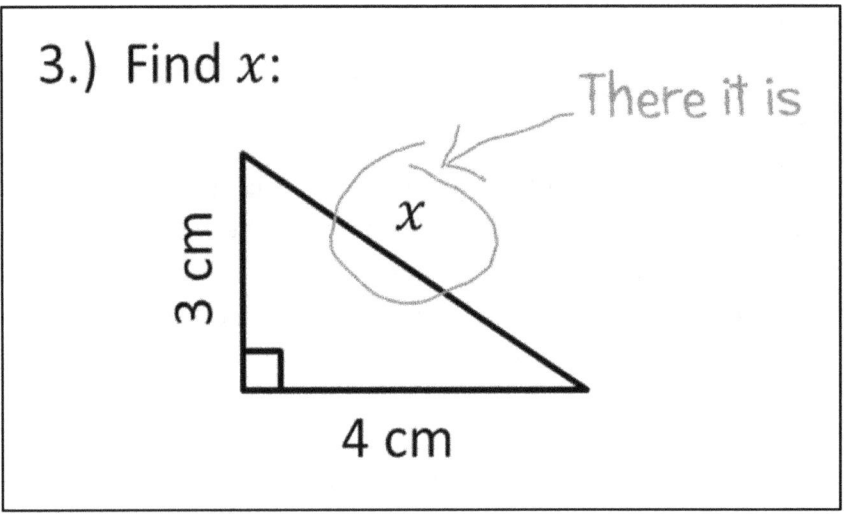

Math in General

The most important thing to know about learning math beyond grade school is that it is about *understanding*, *not memorization*. True, in high school you have to memorize some formulas. The intent being that they are so useful, you won't want to look them up all of the time.

But, notice that when you are tested you don't regurgitate those equations and theorems. Instead, you are expected to know *how to use* the formulas. In college, the emphasis is so heavy on your understanding rather than memorization skills, that many classes allow you to bring the equations with you to the test. Really. Math is very much like a card game. Knowing the rules is not enough. You have to know how to apply the rules in order to win with any hand you are dealt.

The rest of this chapter discusses some ways you can develop better math skills. The best part is that these tips are actually math-free. If you need instruction in math, I've written the NOW 2 kNOW™ Math Series with the following tips in mind, as will be discussed at the end of the chapter.

Logic

To solve an equation in Algebra, find an angle in Geometry, or perform an integral in Calculus, you execute a series of steps that guide you to the correct answer. These steps are built on theorems and postulates with each course building on the material of the prior course. When faced with a math question, these series of steps will eliminate the infinity of possible answers to leave only the correct ones. This process is the application of logic. Logic involves thinking rationally, seeing the big picture, and organizing the details.

Being able to think rationally is an obvious need in mathematics. There are many games that help with getting in the mode of rational thinking like Sudoku, logic puzzles, and Mine Sweep. With these puzzles you are given a small amount of information, and through deduction and knowledge of the rules of the game, you predict the rest. These games do not pit you against another opponent or even chance. There is a final, correct answer, and successful rationalization will get you there. Penny Press publishes a number of books with a variety of such puzzles.

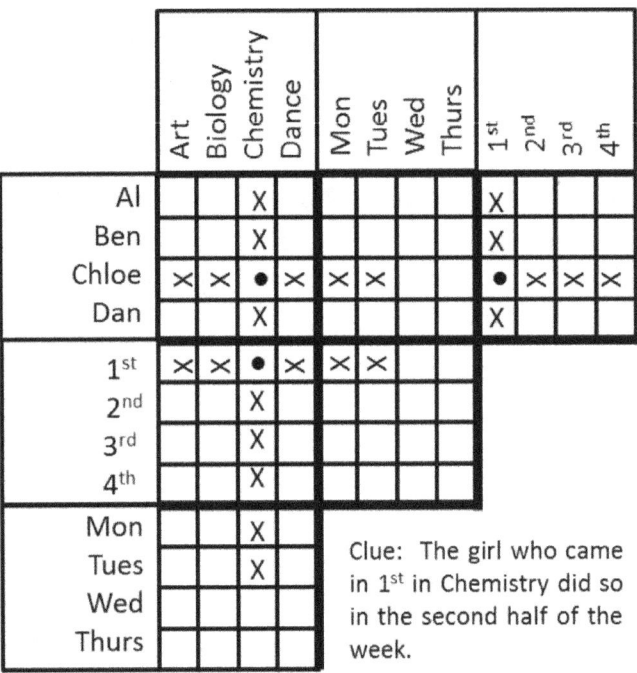

Figure 3-1: Example of using a grid to solve a logic puzzle. The grid matches up possibilities, and we use the clue to mark which must be true (●) and which must be false (X).

Seeing the big picture is a skill that is often overlooked by students. It took me awhile to realize that this skill is extremely effective in my learning style. As I tutored or taught classes, it became obvious that I was not alone. I compare it to navigating a city with a map. A map won't tell you the color of the buildings or the leaves on the trees, but it's good to have a bird's eye view to know where you are. When students are in a typical course, they are bombarded with information and details. It really helps once in a while to step back and make an outline of what has been learned. Write down the key subjects on a single page so you have a snap shot of what's going on. It gives your mind a framework into which you can sort all of the seemingly miscellaneous details. Creating outlines is good for any course, not just math, and also helps when you compose essays or stories.

Finally, organizing the details is a way to keep track of what you are learning in the context of the big picture. For example, when you take Algebra 1, you learn how to factor binomials (problems such as $x^2 + 5x + 4 = (x + 4)(x + 1)$). The idea of factoring binomials is a key concept on your big picture outline. The various methods you use to find the factors are the details that are sorted under that category. To practice, you can try organizing your desk, locker, or closet. Learn how to sort out what's important and find a place for it; discard the rest.

Figure 3-2: A picture of my craft closet.

Bookkeeping

As with any series of steps, you have to be conscious of all of the details from one step to the next. I call this bookkeeping. Bookkeeping is tedious, but it's not a high level skill. Unfortunately, it causes many students to stumble and then lose faith in their math abilities. If you drop a minus sign, it doesn't mean you don't get math. It just means you got a little careless – and it happens to all of us.

In most math courses, you are encouraged to show your work rather than just your final answer, not so much as a check against cheating, but so that you don't lose full credit for a simple mistake. Those mistakes can be frustrating, though, and who wants to lose even one point on a test? Developing better capabilities with tracking details, having confidence, and being patient will help with bookkeeping.

The tracking of details is very important for math since each step towards the answer builds upon the prior one. Learning to pay attention to small details is a skill that can certainly be learned. And, it's helpful in everyday life. Helpful puzzles include finding the difference between pictures and counting the f's in a paragraph. (There are nine in this paragraph.)

Chapter 3: Learning Math

Figure 3-3: Find the six key differences between the two scenes.

Having confidence helps with bookkeeping by keeping you sane. Sometimes students second guess themselves too much and end up creating a black smear across the page with no hope of seeing, let alone tracking, any of the details. As you get better with finding errors in your work or even getting to the end of a problem without errors, be sure to feel more confident in your abilities. Another way to build confidence is to try new things in general. Running, biking, painting, acting, and playing an instrument are a few examples. Just having the courage to try something new can be a confidence builder. Finishing projects also helps build confidence through accomplishment whether it's tackling a chore that's been hanging over your head forever or reading the tome you started last summer. As we'll see in Chapter 6, confidence has a huge impact on standardized testing results. When students are told they should expect to do well (or poorly), they tend to rise (or fall) to the occasion dramatically.

Finally, being patient helps enormously with bookkeeping. As I said before, bookkeeping is tedious. A speedy mentality is not helpful here. Meditation, yoga, slow breathing, and spending quiet time with pets can all help to teach patience and calm on demand.

Pattern Seeking

Identifying patterns is a key skill in math. As stated at the beginning of this chapter, math is about understanding, not memorization. You are tested on how well you can use a formula rather than how well you can memorize it. In order to do this successfully, you have to know which formula or technique to use. That's where pattern recognition comes in. The sooner you can figure out the right approach, the sooner you get the problem solved. Seeing the big picture helps you to understand when to use what you've learned. For instance, if asked to factor a binomial, you would use the tools you learned for that rather than tools that help you solve inequalities. In addition, word problems are ripe for pattern recognition. Once you realize "and" means "add" and "of" means "multiply" you are well on your way to a solution. The keys to success are spotting similarities, finding hidden patterns, and using tools creatively.

Spotting similarities is the first step in pattern recognition. When you do a certain kind of problem over and over again, you start to notice similarities in the way the problems are phrased or laid out. These similarities will cue you in the future to what techniques can be used successfully. That's why you get lots of math homework. It gives you practice and helps you find the patterns. Another way to improve your capabilities is to do jigsaw puzzles. To complete jigsaws, you study the edges of the pieces to see similar colors, patterns, or shapes. Similarly, solving cryptograms (sentences that have been written with a replacement alphabet) helps enhance your ability to see patterns.

To solve the cryptogram of Figure 3-4, you would start with the small words guessing "the," "and," "of," and "is" then work on repeated words or characters.

```
F B N J M J Q   X Y   F D Q J G J Y Y   K X Z B   Z B J

Z Q P Z B   X W   Y H D G G   H D Z Z J Q Y   F D W W N Z

S J   Z Q P Y Z J A   K X Z B   X H C N Q Z D W Z

H D Z Z J Q Y :     D G S J Q Z   J X W Y Z J X W .
```

Figure 3-4: A cryptogram of a quote followed by the author's name.

Finding hidden patterns is taking your skills to the next level, and it's extremely useful in math. As one example, when you work a word problem, you need to strip away all of the "story-telling" words and get to the meat of the problem – the resulting equation. From there it's easy to solve. In another example, you may have to simplify the components in a given equation to get it into a form that is recognizable to you. Humans are great at finding patterns and coming up with general rules. Proverbs like "waste not, want not" and "a stitch in time saves nine" can be applied to many kinds of situations (just like one formula or technique can apply to many math problems). Think of things that have happened in your life. Have you made up any rules that keep you from repeating mistakes should a similar set of circumstances occur? Sorting the chaos of life is about finding hidden patterns.

Using tools creatively is almost like pattern seeking in reverse. The principle here is to see if basic tools can be used in new ways to achieve successful results. If you get stuck solving a problem because you can't remember the most recent formula, you may be able to go back to basics and try older techniques. Sometimes being able to get creative with the basics is the most effective way to get to the answer. In trigonometry, I found it was far more beneficial for me to remember a few formulas and derive the rest on the fly rather than try to memorize tons of equations (which would provide ample opportunity to make mistakes).

To practice this skill, let's say you want to build a bird house but have limited tools. With your hammer, you can obviously drive nails. And, if you make a mistake, the hammer can double as a crowbar. But, if you need to make a mark, you could use the claw to scribe the wood. You could use portions of the hammer for rough measurements. When creating a painting, many artists use only a few base colors to mix as needed and a small set of brushes used creatively for different effects. There are many kinds of projects that lend themselves well to working creatively with a small set of tools.

Abstraction

Abstraction is the ability think outside of the box, as they say. Geometry, word problems, applied math, engineering, and physics are areas that rely on abstract thinking. Artists, writers, and musicians as well as mathematicians, engineers, and scientists use their right brains to see things clearly others see as complex or chaotic. Don't worry if you are not an artist or a mathematician (yet). Abstraction can be learned through seeing new perspectives, anticipating the next thing, and improving spatial reasoning as outlined below.

There are so many ways to see new perspectives and expand your way of looking at everyday things. Sit upside down and imagine walking through your home as though it were flipped. Read or create metaphors and similes about everyday experiences. Answer or create

"Who Am I" riddles that stretch your reasoning skills. Even attempting to see the world from someone else's perspective such as a child, a partner, or a friend, can help you expand your mind outside of the proverbial box.

Anticipating the next thing is a powerful strategy in any life situation. Knowing the world has predictable rules helps us not only to solve problems but to create desired outcomes no matter how overwhelming all of the possibilities may seem. In Algebra, for example, we often tend to work backwards – knowing we want x on one side of the equation, and figuring out the needed steps. In life, we set lofty goals for ourselves and then work backward to figure out the steps that will get us there. Playing chess is a great way to learn strategy. But, if chess isn't your game, or if you are working on these skills alone, solving mazes or answering SAT next-in-series questions will help develop the ability to see the path of predicted outcomes to get to the final answer.

I have an eye but can't see; I'm fierce and fast but have no legs. What am I?	Clock Time Barometer Pressure Scale Mass Thermometer _____

Figure 3-5: Examples of Who Am I riddle and Next-in-series.

Finally, improving spatial reasoning is a great asset for subjects like geometry or physics and for doing well on standardized math tests like the SAT, ACT, and GRE. In particular, the ability to do mental rotations, imagining an object from different angles, is a great tool. As we'll see in Chapter 6, spatial reasoning can be learned in a variety of ways. Playing video games, engaging in sports, and building things all help develop this aspect of our brains. For me, I found it helpful to attempt to draw or paint in near photographic realism.

When Will I Ever Need Math?

Once more, I must praise the merits of math. Many a student asks, "When will I ever need math?" Well, let's just ignore opening the door to high paying careers and enabling new technologies that help us live longer, have more comforts, and be more interconnected as human beings.

The basic skills needed for math helps us on a daily, personal basis. Let's review what the various math skills can help us do in "real" life:

Logic:
- Think rationally and objectively about problems presented to us and understand that there is a systematic way to resolve issues.
- See the big picture to determine if we like where we are and where we are going.
- Organize the chaos in our world.

Bookkeeping:
- See the details in life that we may have formerly taken for granted.
- Build self-confidence in our problem solving skills and with that an increased sense of independence and self-reliance.
- Develop the ability to enjoy moments of calm and quiet contemplation.

Pattern Seeking:

- Identify common threads in life to find solutions more quickly.
- Develop rules that help avoid future pitfalls based on past mistakes.
- Be creative enough to handle new tasks with the tools we have on hand.

Abstraction:

- Understand another person's perspective more deeply.
- Work backward from goals to define a successful path to our ideals.
- Improve our video game, athletic, or toy building prowess. ☺

The NOW 2 kNOW™ Math Series

As mentioned in the beginning of this chapter, I've written a series of math books to help students with the above tips in mind. The NOW 2 kNOW™ Math series is written differently than most texts. The problem sets are at the end of the book so that the course material can flow logically from one chapter to the next. The material is thorough, but the delivery is concise so that an entire subject can be explained in 80 pages or less. The important information is highlighted so that you can easily identify what is worth remembering, what is explanatory information, and what is an illustrative example. This helps identify the important details. I recall my first math texts were almost yellow with highlighting as I worried I might overlook some important tidbit.

The first appendix is a course outline on a two page spread that gives the all-in-one-glance big picture summary. The following appendices include over 200 problems with worked out solutions that can be used as personal tests or further examples. Including so many problem sets helps build recognition and familiarity with the techniques, gives plenty of practice with bookkeeping, and illustrates new ways of applying the learned material. I remember being a student and spending an hour on a problem to try to match the book solution only to discover in class the next day that the author made a mistake. I'm not infallible, either, so by showing my work you can figure out if you or I made a mistake when a discrepancy exists in our answers.

The series is available on Amazon.com or at www.NOW2kNOW.com. If these books don't feel like a good fit for you, I encourage you to seek help from your instructor, a tutor, a parent, the internet, a different set of books, etc. The most important thing is to keep the math door open on your future!

Answers to the Riddles

Figure 3-3:   Missing ornament, smaller trunk, smaller box, shorter fireplace opening, moved stocking, and candle on mantle.

Figure 3-4:   Whoever is careless with the truth in small matters cannot be trusted with important matters: Albert Einstein.

Figure 3-5a: Hurricane

Figure 3-5b: Temperature

Chapter 4: The Costs of College

You may have seen reports or know people who say that college is a scam that cripples graduates with debt. This is not true of all colleges and all majors. Yes, people who major in a field without realizing that they need a Master's or Doctorate to find a decent paying job will graduate with high debt and an unmarketable degree.

Also, people who go to an outlandishly priced school may find the increased debt outweighs whatever increased starting salary their expensive school promised. Keep in mind, too, that by and large, your mid-career salary is dictated more by your performance and experience than by the name of the school you attended in your early 20's. If you decide to go to graduate school, many STEM fields offer free tuition allowing you to then base your decision on name rather than cost.

The bottom line is this: College is nothing more than a vocational school like Lincoln Tech or ITT; its main purpose is to train you for a job!

A Breakdown of College Costs

There are many considerations in choosing a college or university. First and foremost, you must make sure it is accredited and offers your selected major. It's a good idea to see if they have many fields of study as most freshmen change their majors. Second, ask the school about their job placement statistics in your target career. They should be bragging about those statistics and have them at the ready! Third, if you are paying for it, make sure you can afford it in the long haul. That question is what this chapter will address.

Tuition is the base cost for attending a college. Tuition can be higher for certain majors including STEM when variable tuition is implemented [1]. A big factor on cost is whether you are going to school in your home state (in-state) or another state (out-of-state). Most public schools offer significantly reduced tuition for in-state students. Variable tuition and in-state reductions should be clearly laid out on any school's website. In addition, fees are also charged to cover a variety of things like administrative costs and gym access. Sometimes health insurance and bus access are also included in fees.

If you won't be living in free accommodations while attending school, e.g. living with a generous relative, then you will also have to pay room and board (lodging and food). There are generally two choices: living on-campus or living off-campus. Many 4-year schools will require incoming freshman to live on-campus the first year. The benefits of doing so are usually decreased and fixed expenses as well as the chance to interact socially with other classmates.

Eventually, you may want to move off-campus, but be aware that rents may be higher and meals and utilities will be unknown, variable expenses to your budget. If you move off-campus, you should probably expect about a 30-50% increase in room and board expenses compared to living on-campus. In addition, you will want to determine if you can sublet, or rent your place to someone else, over the summer months if you don't plan to live in your apartment then. Otherwise, you will be required to pay rent and utilities for an additional three months of the year.

Figure 4-1 gives the average breakdown of annual costs for tuition and fees as well as room and board (for on-campus students) for the 2014-15 school year [2]. These costs reflect full-time enrollment. Part-time attendance can reduce the tuition portion of your expenses. As you can see, there is a significant cost advantage to attending community college the first two years or attending public school as an in-state student.

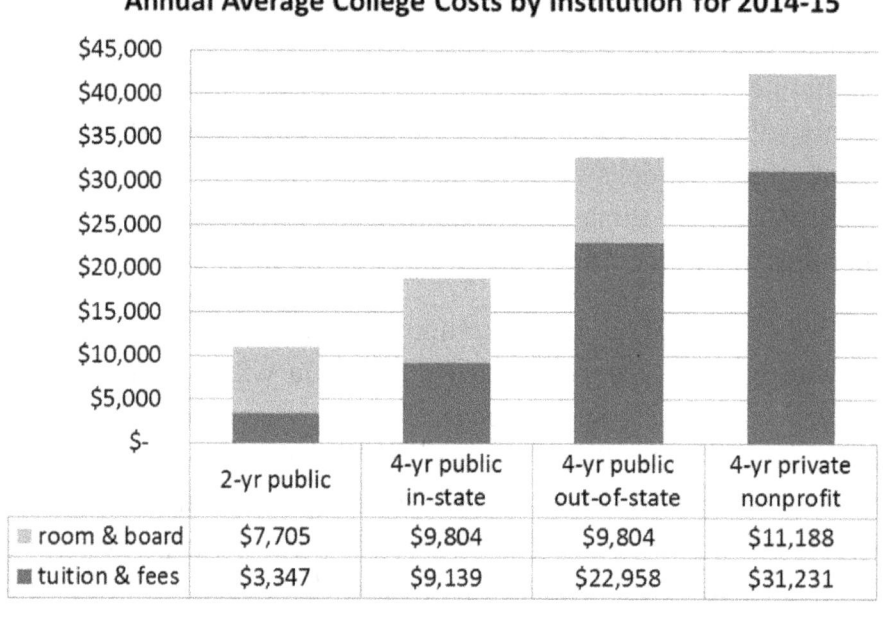

Figure 4-1: Average college costs by institution for the 2014-15 school year [2].

Tuition, fees, room, and board are certainly the biggest components of the price of college, but there are other costs to consider:

1. Books and supplies – estimate $1200 per year [1]
2. Health Insurance (if not included in fees or paid by someone else on your behalf could run ~$2200 per year [3])
3. Car (insurance and gas) or bus fare (if not included in fees)
4. Phone plan
5. Spending money - $100/mo isn't much for pizza, vices,, etc.
6. One-time costs – computer, equipment, desk

You are typically looking at $13,000 - $22,000 per year before considering transportation, phone plans, and spending money. If you feel terrified, you are not alone. This is why it's so important to make careful choices about majors and schools. It doesn't make much sense to spend this kind of money and end up in a worse financial situation.

Paying for College

Now let's look at how students pay for college. The two main avenues are military and civilian. Military options are (as outlined in detail at http://www.myfuture.com/military/articles-advice/college-assistance):

- Before service
    - Reserve Officers' Training Program (ROTC) (see http://www.military.com/rotc)
    - Service academies or military colleges
- During service
    - Coursework while enlisted in the military
- After service
    - GI bill and other funds

All of the above options provide the opportunity to receive full tuition, room, board, medical, and book expenses. The before service options provide regular college instruction as well as leadership courses that train the student to be an officer.

If scholarships are accepted, the student is required to complete 4-5 years of service upon graduation. The ROTC program is available at over 1100 colleges across the U.S., or you can attend a service academy or military college (like the U.S. Naval Academy). Programs are available in the Army, Air Force, and Naval branches of the military.

There are many programs for enlisted personnel that allow college study during service. Assistance is based on years of active duty and other eligibility requirements. As an enlisted person, room and board are already covered along with a salary.

For those who have already served in active duty in the last 15 years, the GI bill provides financial assistance for college. Each military branch also supports college fund programs for additional help.

The military route rightfully scares some people because of the commitment to service, but it does ensure you have a job when you graduate and can eliminate having to start your adult life burdened with debt. Know, too, that students can enroll in part of the "before service" options for the leadership training without accepting scholarship money to avoid service requirements. It may then be possible to secure an officer position upon graduation.

There are also three civilian options:

- Scholarships for special abilities, interests, or achievements
    - Check out http://www.collegescholarships.org/ and http://www.studentscholarships.org/
- Need-based grants and loans
    - Fill out the Free Application for Federal Student Aid (FAFSA) which you can find at https://fafsa.ed.gov/
- Stafford loans (also must fill out the FAFSA)

The first two options are competitive, and many students don't qualify. Most students end up going the third route: Stafford loans. Stafford loans are granted to U.S. citizens, permanent residents, and eligible non-citizens who are enrolled in college at least half time. Unless you are in default (not making expected payments) on a current school loan, credit is not a factor on receiving the loan, and you don't need a cosigner (a credit-worthy person willing to pay the loan if you do not).

There are two types of Stafford loans: Subsidized and Unsubsidized. Both types of loans are for tuition, housing, food, books, and required expenses. Both types of loans do not require you to pay anything until six months after you are no longer enrolled at least half time. You can also request additional deferments (excused periods of non-payment) upon certain conditions. The difference in the two types of loans is:

- For subsidized loans, the federal government pays the interest on the loan while you are in school. When you graduate, you owe what you borrowed and start paying the interest yourself.

- For unsubsidized loans, you have the choice of paying interest while in school or capitalizing the interest until you graduate. Capitalizing means interest is continually added to your original loan amount (principle). You will then owe more than you borrowed when you graduate.

There are limits to how much you can borrow based on your year in school and whether or not you are independent. Gaining independent status unfortunately has nothing do with whether you are financially independent. You are considered independent if you meet certain criteria outlined at https://studentaid.ed.gov/fafsa/filling-out/dependency. For most students, the major criteria are:

- You are over 24 years old,
- You are a court emancipated minor, or
- You are married or supporting children, or
- You were under court ordered legal guardianship or were a ward of the state (not incarcerated) after you turned 13 years old, or
- Your parents are incarcerated, missing, or other.

In general, if you are not considered independent, your parents' financial information is taken into account on the FAFSA to determine if you qualify for need-based grants and loans. You also must be independent to get a subsidized Stafford loan.

For many, the unsubsidized Stafford loan is the only way to go (you still need to fill out the FAFSA every year you take out a new loan). The limits of borrowing in a given year for any Stafford loan are listed below [4]. If you qualify for subsidized loans, a portion of the loan limit will be eligible, but not all. The difference is then made up in unsubsidized loans.

Year in School	1	2	3+	Total Allowed
Dependent	$5,500	$6,500	$7,500	$31,000
Independent	$9,500	$10,500	$12,500	$57,500

Figure 4-2: Loan limits for the federal Stafford loan for undergraduate study [4].

If graduate school is in your future, aim for the best school you can get into that will still pay your tuition if that is available in your field of study. If you borrow, the following table gives the annual and total limits [4]:

	Annual	Total Including Undergraduate
Graduate School	$20,500	$138,500
Medical School	$40,500	$224,000

Figure 4-3: Loan limits for the federal Stafford loan for graduate study [4].

How then, you may ask, does a "dependent" student facing up to $22,000 in annual costs pay for the first year with a mere $5,500 loan? First, keep in mind that the costs listed in the preceding section are averages. That means that half of the schools out there charge less than average – sometimes by a lot. Also, if you can find a cosigner, banks will offer additional personal loans for school. The interest rates and terms of payment will vary with the bank used. There are other tips to consider, as well.

If you are deemed "dependent" because your family earns more than the minimum qualifications, your parents (biological or adoptive) may take out a PLUS loan for you. Divorced parents can each request a PLUS loan. The loan has higher interest rates with a 10-year repayment term, requires good credit or a cosigner, and is not extended to any other member of the family [5]. The loans are meant to cover the entire cost of an undergraduate program minus any aid given from other sources. If your parents to do not qualify for a PLUS loan, your unsubsidized Stafford loan limits are extended to the "independent" student limits.

For various reasons, some parents may not be willing to incur debt even if they would qualify for a PLUS loan (despite a promise from you to repay). That would keep you under the "dependent" student loan limits, so saving as much money as possible becomes even more important. Many students start at community college the first two years to keep costs down. Some states, such as California, Pennsylvania, and Minnesota, and some schools in Wisconsin and Indiana offer aid to middle-class students who don't qualify for academic or athletic scholarships [6]. Also, in-state tuition is incredibly helpful if you can go to school within your state. Your college web site will list in-state costs if they offer them.

If you need to move out of state, you may be able to achieve in-state status. This usually requires one year residency, a driver's license, not being claimed on your parents' tax return, and working and filing taxes in the new state. There are usually minimums you have to earn with a cap on how much can be given to you by relatives. It may sound complicated, but I did it in Virginia, so it can be done. Your school website should list eligibility requirements for gaining in-state tuition.

Also remember that you can work summers to help offset costs. You might want to work while in school, but be warned that college will tax your time unlike anything you've ever seen in high school. It may be wise to go half-time if you plan to work while in school – at least until you get the hang of it. Or, you may decide to take a semester off here and there to earn some cash waiting tables or working in retail. In STEM, you have the option in later years to work in what is sometimes called cooperative education. This means that you work for a real company in your field as a trainee every other semester. You gain real experience and earn much more than minimum wage. Since you have six months before you have to pay on your loans, a return to school the following semester resets the payment clock. I personally used all of the above techniques.

Other options that may help are living at home while going to school, cutting unnecessary expenses, or giving up your car for bus transportation. Some people also complete a two year program that lands a good job, like radiation therapist or engineering technician. If they decide to go for additional degrees, some employers will actually pay the tuition in return for staying with the company for some years afterward. This may entail going to night school while working full-time, splitting time between work and school, or even returning to school full-time.

Making College Pay Off

We started this chapter with the question - can you afford school *for the long haul*? Let's say you manage to graduate with a Bachelor's degree in your chosen field. What are your expenses? How much do you have to pay in school loans? What will you earn to offset these costs?

Just as in college, you will need money for rent, food, and utilities as well as money for the phone, car, and spending. If you know where you will live in the U.S., you can use http://www.bestplaces.net/ to estimate cost of living. As a rule of thumb, the average rent for a one bedroom apartment in the U.S. is ~$800/month [7]. Utilities ($300), food ($500), phone ($100), car and insurance ($300), and spending money ($200) easily get you to about $2,200/month in expenses.

As for school loans, consider the worst case example. Let's say you were a "dependent" student that took 5 years to graduate and borrowed the full amount of $31,000 without making any payments thus far. With a 5% interest rate, you now owe just over $36,000. The loans have a 10 year repayment term once you are out of school, so you can expect to pay ~$450/month (a total of $54,000 when you are done).

If you were an independent student that borrowed $57,500 over 5 years, and for ease of calculation let's assume the unlikely case that none of the loans were subsidized, you now owe ~$67,000 with a loan payment of ~$800/month (you'll pay $96,000 in the end).

You can save significant money in the long run by paying more than the minimum each month, but we'll start with the numbers given. You need to take home $2,650-$3,000 per month in pay, depending on your circumstances.

So, how much can you expect to earn? Well, you'll be starting out, so expect to be toward the lower end of the income bracket of your chosen field. Good estimates can be obtained at www.myfuture.com or in *NOW 2 kNOW™ High Paying Careers in STEM*. Take 1/3 of that out for taxes and benefits. Benefits include low cost medical plans and contributions to your 401k should you choose to do so.

If we work backwards, a person needing to clear $2650/mo should aim to make $48,000 per year. If you need $3000/mo, then aim for $55,000 per year. You can quickly see why an unmarketable degree is bad news.

Using the examples above, you can start to estimate what tuition costs seem reasonable for your chosen career. These are not hard and fast numbers. Your living expenses after college don't have to be so high, and you may not have to borrow the full maximum amounts.

Finally, you may also consider if going to graduate school is a wise choice for you. You won't have to pay your loans for a bit longer, and your pay should be higher when you get out. This makes sense if you are in a major where you can go to school for free and/or with a small stipend to help with your cost of living. Otherwise, weigh the anticipated salary with the additional accumulated debt.

So, yes, college is expensive in addition to being hard. But, there are ways to pay for it. The military options can get you through debt-free to a paying job. The loan route is doable as long as you plan carefully. But, skipping college or some other training program altogether is the harder path in the long term. If you want to clear $2200/month to live comfortably without college, you need to find something that pays $40,000 per year (~$20/hour) and includes benefits. That is hard to do with only a high school degree.

References

[1] Collegedata.com. "What's the Price Tag for a College Education?" *Collegedata: Pay Your Way*: http://www.collegedata.com/cs/content/content_payarticle_tmpl.jhtml?articleId=10064.

[2] CollegeBoard.org. "Trends in Higher Education: Average Published Undergraduate Charges by Sector, 2014-15," *Trends in Higher Education*. CollegeBoard.org: http://trends.collegeboard.org/college-pricing/figures-tables/average-published-undergraduate-charges-sector-2014-15.

[3] Ann Carrns. "For College Students, So Many Plans to Choose From," *The New York Times: Financial Planners*. August 22, 2013: http://trends.collegeboard.org/college-pricing/figures-tables/average-published-undergraduate-charges-sector-2014-15.

[4] StaffordLoan.com: http://www.staffordloan.com/stafford-loan-info/stafford-loan-limits.php.

[5]   Kantrowitz, Mark. "Introduction to Federal Parent PLUS Loans," *Edvisors*: https://www.edvisors.com/college-loans/federal/parent-plus/introduction-to-federal-parent-plus-loans/.

[6]   Korn, Melissa. "Colleges' New Aid Target: The Middle Class," *The Wall Street Journal*. December 30, 2014: http://www.wsj.com/articles/colleges-new-aid-target-the-middle-class-1419894937.

[7]   Sperling's Best Places: http://www.bestplaces.net.

Chapter 5: Getting Through College

There are many, many things that go into surviving college other than just paying for it. In a STEM field, the work is challenging and fast paced. Unfortunately, most of our high schools do not prepare us for the enormous workloads, the autonomy, and the real chance at failure in college. I went to a very good high school and found that to be the case.

College is just one step away from the "real world" where life can be hard and unforgiving at times. Your job is to get through so that you have the financial stability to weather future storms more easily. And, the skills you master to get through college are the same ones that will help you in life.

This chapter gives information on the logistics of undergraduate and graduate school. It also offers some pointers on survival tactics that I personally have found very helpful.

Undergraduate School - Logistics

On the logistics side of an undergraduate program, you have to make decisions on what kind of degree to get, what school to choose, and where to live. Degrees range from 2-year Associate's Degrees to 4-year Bachelor's Degrees. The amount of math and science taken dictate whether you will get a Bachelor's of Science, B.S., or a Bachelor's of Art, B.A. In STEM, you'll be getting a B.S. if you go the four years. Your choice of career dictates if you need an A.S., B.S., or additional degrees and certifications.

When choosing your school, cost and job placement should be key factors as discussed in Chapter 4. However, there are other considerations, as well. Many students change majors in their first or second year, so you may want a school that offers more than just your number one choice. The first year or two are often generic enough that changing from one STEM major to a related major won't cost you much time. This is also why community college is a great, low cost way to get your more generalized courses out of the way.

The size of a college or university may also be important to you. A large school may offer more resources like a bigger library or better technology, but a small school will offer smaller classes and individual attention. You may also want to consider whether the campus has its own graduate, medical, or veterinary school. Preference is often given to accepting students who are alumni of the school's own undergraduate programs.

The choice to live on- or off-campus is one that may be determined your first year by your school or financial situation. Unless your family lives close to the college, you may be expected to stay on-campus in a residence hall the first year to help you get acclimated. This is actually good practice as it forces you to meet fellow students and makes forming study groups a little easier. After the first year or two, however, you may prefer the quiet of off-campus housing despite the probable increase in costs.

As you progress through your undergraduate program, there are two other logistical aspects to keep in mind. First, never assume that if you fill out a form or do what is asked that the administration will do their part. Things get lost, people get busy, and life just happens. Always follow up to make sure the FAFSA got filed, the tuition got paid, and the classes you asked for were given to you. Don't be afraid to go in person and talk to people. That's how stuff gets done, and that's also the way you find out that rules are just guidelines. An in person visit will many times result in a short cut that other students don't know about.

Second, if your major offers a cooperative education program think seriously about it. The cooperative education program gives you the opportunity to work for a company in your field every other semester. The school will work with you to get interviews and arrange your coursework. It will take you an extra year to graduate, but you will have experience to put on your job or graduate school application, the pay is much better than minimum wage, and your exposure to industry will help make your studies more meaningful.

Choosing a College

Accredited in Your Major
Good Job Placement in Your Major
Affordable

Other Areas of Study Offered
School Size (Resources/Teacher-Student Ratio)
On-Campus Grad or Med School
Near or Away from Home
Cooperative Education Available

Figure 5-1: A few considerations for choosing a college.

Undergraduate School - Survival

On the survival side of the undergraduate program, you need to learn how to stay sane, how to self-regulate, and how to get good grades. The one thing that often surprises people is the sheer amount of work that is required. I didn't encounter too many professors that seemed to care that I had other classes assigning heavy workloads, too. And, the first two years are the worst with "weed out" classes that seem designed to make you fail.

You need to realize that there are times when you absolutely cannot do it all. This is especially true if you are also working while going to school. The key is to prioritize. You may have to skip a homework assignment for 5% of your grade so that you can study harder for a test that makes up 20% of your grade. As you progress in your studies, you'll learn how to study and work more efficiently, and this will all become second nature. But, in the beginning, don't beat up on yourself too much if you need to skip a lab assignment.

Staying sane also means making time for friends and diversions. You may know people in other majors that seem to have boatloads of free time, and you don't want to miss out on all of the fun. Colleges offer many great experiences and work hard to provide opportunities for a good student life. Just be aware that you have to temper this with some degree of self-regulation.

College can be very autonomous, i.e. you are in control of whether you succeed or fail. Many students are ill-prepared for such a free environment where no one is making sure you did your work or showed up for class. It can be extremely difficult to stay indoors to study when there are people having fun just outside your window. I remember dreading spring time for just that reason year after year (now I love the season).

You have to know what you need to do to succeed and remind yourself that your perseverance will pay off. College is a vocational school that prepares you for a job, not a once-in-a-lifetime, multi-year party. It is possible to achieve balance, to have fun, and to still get good grades.

Speaking of grades, it may be hard at first to figure out just what it is that you need to succeed. Many courses are graded on a curve. If you are not familiar with that term, it means you are graded relative to everyone else. The median of the students are assigned a C, and the rest of the grades are divvied out so that there are fewer B's and D's and even fewer A's and F's. I once took a physics course where the average overall grade for the course was 25%. Yes, a 25% got you a C grade for the course.

I mention grading on a curve for a couple of reasons. One, if a course is particularly hard, an absolute, low score may still be a relative, good score, and it's the latter that counts. Two, other students know this, so they will study all night to beat you out. Some are even a little evil about it. There was a course I took where days before each test, this one student would talk loudly before the professor came in, standing so everyone could hear him "talking to his friend." He would declare that the material was so easy that he didn't think he was going to bother to study. In reality, he was hoping to undermine other students' confidences and trick the lazy ones into not studying, as well. I would bet a year's pay he studied all night for every one of those exams.

Managing the curve is one aspect to getting good grades, and another is learning how to study. It took me a while to learn what worked for me. Eventually, I went from freezing up and totally blanking on exams to finishing first with some of the highest grades. The two things that worked for me were organizing the information and studying a little every night. I got pretty good about looking at the big picture of the course every so often. The practice helped me figure out what kinds of problems required what kinds of solutions, and it helped me keep track of all of the details.

I also found that studying every night or so in each class helped immensely. I would look over my notes and read the text making sure that I *understood* the material. By doing this regularly, I could ask questions about gaps in my knowledge sooner than later. Further, the night before the exam became a simple exercise of flipping through my notes to find the one or two things I was weak on. This helped with time management around a last minute change in work schedule, and it also helped build my confidence during exam time. Cramming was definitely not something that worked for me.

Other ways students survive college courses is by forming study groups that work on homework together. Be careful not to just copy answers from others but actually understand the work. You will be tested on it. But, most STEM courses encourage students to work together as it can spark discussion that enhances understanding of the material.

You should also take advantage of the professor or assistant teacher office hours as needed. They are there to help you learn, and most really do care about you succeeding. They will be much more patient, though, if you don't wait to the last minute to join the herd of 100 other students vying to ask them questions.

And, please go to class. I was arrogant enough at first to think I could just read the assigned text and show up for exams. What actually happens, though, is that the professor isn't reading the text along with the class year after year. Professors teach from their own notes and their own ideas of what is important. That's also what they test you on; the text is just supplementary material. If you think the professor is an idiot, show up, keep one ear open, and do your other work quietly in the back of the class. You never know when you'll be tested on some pearl that was discussed.

Along these lines, pay attention to your note taking. In so many classes, I would see the professor talking through some really important stuff, but no one else wrote anything down until it was on the board. As much as you can, stay engaged in class and check your understanding as the hour progresses. Write down what seems important or what you might forget later, whether the professor bothered to write it on the board or not.

My final bit of advice on getting the grade is to show your work on exams. As an assistant teacher, I used to joke that I was grading mathematical essays, with a lead sentence, supporting information, and a conclusion. If there was a simple sign error early on, I made sure to follow the student's subsequent steps to see if the reasoning held. If a simple arithmetic error was the cause for a completely wrong answer, it only cost the student a point. But, if all I had to go on was the wrong answer, I might have to deduct most or all of the 20 points for not demonstrating knowledge of the material.

Surviving Undergrad

Prioritize Your Time
Find Balance Between Work and Fun
Learn What It Takes For You to Succeed
Remember Why You are There
Manage the Grading Curve
Organize Information
Review Course Notes Regularly
Form or Join Study Groups
Seek Professor/T.A. Help
Go To Class
Take Great Notes
Show Your Work

FIND YOUR FIRE!

Figure 5-2: Tips for surviving undergraduate study.

Before I leave this section, there is one other survival tool that is key to undergraduate programs. That key is fire. They will throw impossible workloads, ridiculous demands, and sometimes even insults at you. You may get so tired and frustrated that all you want to do is sleep for a week. You may believe that Professor Jackass has it in for you personally. Just remember why you are going through all of this. Remember Chapter 1. You deserve a good future. I remember a couple of courses where I sat in the back and stared at the professor thinking silently, but fiercely, "you will not stand in my way!" Find your fire.

Graduate School - Logistics

Depending on your chosen profession, graduate school may be a way increase your career options, as in engineering, or it may be a necessity, as in some medical fields. A Ph.D. is required if you want to be a college professor. No matter the case, your attendance at graduate school puts you in a higher loan limit category if you need to pay for school, and it keeps you in a deferred payment status for existing school loans.

In the medical fields, there are usually specialty schools offering specific degrees in pharmacy, optometry, medicine, veterinary science, etc. Most schools are extremely competitive, so it's a good idea to look at your wish list of schools a few years in advance as competition may steer you toward one specialty or another. There are several medical programs that only require two years of undergraduate study, but most will prefer a full four year degree in biology, chemistry, or related to attend.

To get into a medical program, you'll need to pass the Medical College Admissions Test (MCAT), the Dental Aptitude Test (DAT), or similar depending on your specialty. You may also need to apply through the

American Medical College Application Service (AMCAS), and perhaps pass an interview process. Once in, your program will phase from course and lab work to mainly patient interactions. At some point, usually in your second year, you need to pass additional examinations to continue your studies.

The graduate program will require anywhere from 2 – 4 years of study and 1 – 10 years of internship or residency, depending on the specialty. Passing a national exam to complete certification and licensing is also generally required before working as a medical professional.

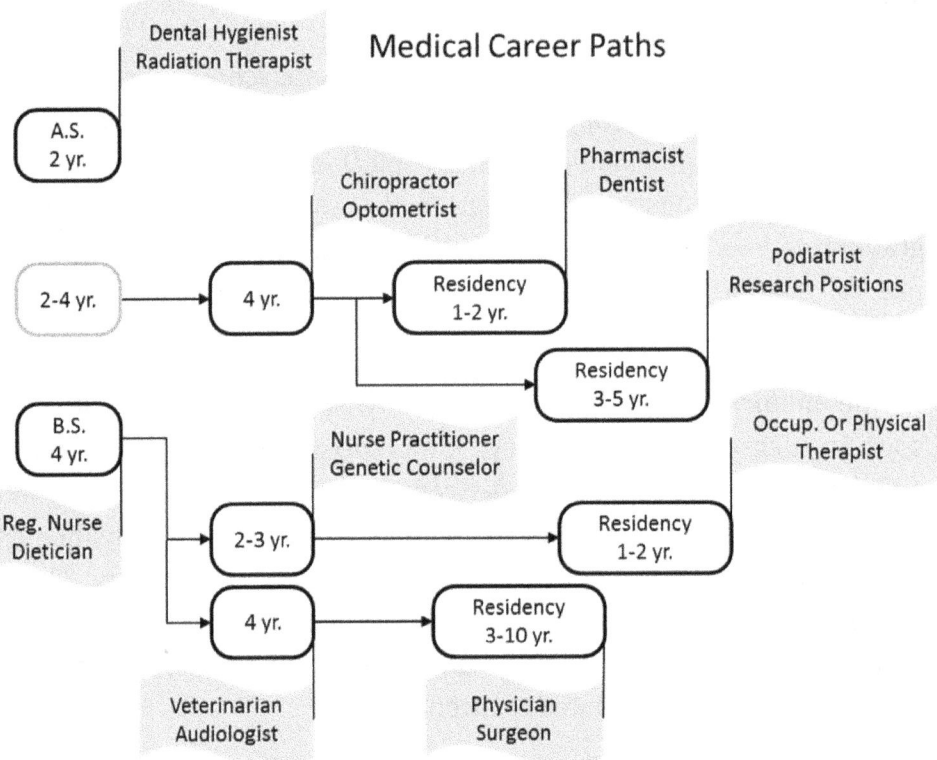

Figure 5-3: Possible medical career paths with sample careers shown. Licensing or certifications are required to practice in medical professions.

In the other STEM fields, graduate school follows a full four year B.S. program in a technical field of study. Your graduate major and undergraduate major might not be the same if they are related enough. This gives some additional flexibility in building your resume. To apply to graduate school, you need to take the Graduate Research Examination (GRE) which is much like the SAT or ACT. You'll also need letters of recommendation much like applying for undergrad. You generally have three choices for the graduate degree: the Master's degree with or without a thesis option and the Ph.D. Some schools combine the M.S. and Ph.D. programs.

The Master's program typically takes 1 ½ - 2 years to complete. The non-thesis option is heavier in coursework, whereas the thesis option will require a few classes while you complete a research project. The research project culminates in a dissertation or thesis paper (a 50-150 page detailed report) and a defense of your research to a panel of professors. The panel of professors includes your advisor, the one with whom you work closely and receive funds for your research, and your committee members, usually 2 -3 other professors who can also give guidance. The thesis option is the one to choose if you wish to go directly into the Ph.D. program afterward. If you plan to work in industry for some time before contemplating the Ph.D., your work experience may compensate for a non-thesis M.S. degree.

The Ph.D. program also requires coursework and a research project. Typical programs last 4 years, unless you are getting the combined M.S./Ph.D. which will take 5 – 6 years after the B.S. The combined program is ideal if you know you want to go all of the way as it will typically require only one research project. In either case, the thesis paper is usually longer, and the committee may be larger.

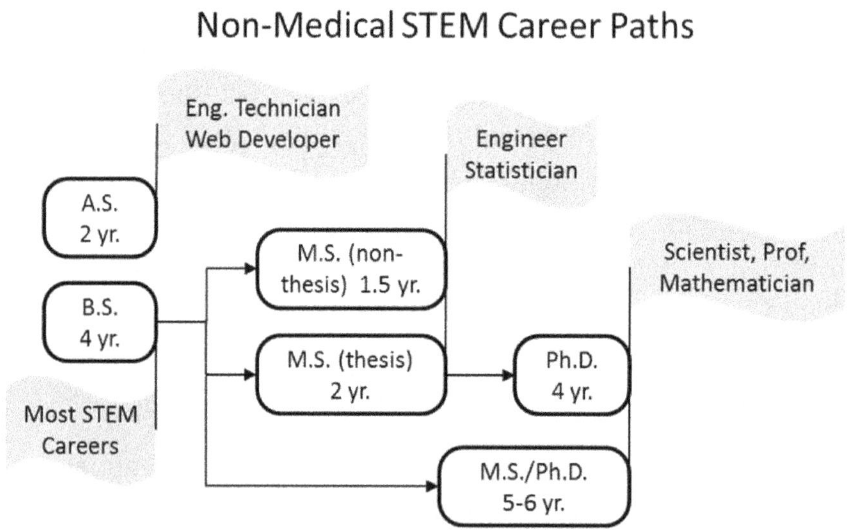

Non-Medical STEM Career Paths

Figure 5-4: Sample non-medical STEM career paths with sample careers shown.

Getting through the Ph.D. program requires up to three written or oral exams. The qualifier exam is taken some time in the first year or two to determine if you will be able to continue. If you are in the combined program, you may be encouraged to stop at the M.S. degree based on the results of the qualifier. There may be an intermediary exam to check the validity of your research project and make any necessary corrections. Finally, there is the defense which is the oral presentation of your research to your advisor and the rest of your committee.

In terms of paying for graduate school, many of the non-medical STEM fields will have opportunities to attend school with tuition paid. Many also offer stipends or small salaries for half-time work while you attend. The stipend typically comes in two forms: the teaching assistantship (T.A.) and the research assistantship (R.A.). You may get one or the other for the semesters you are enrolled, and you may even switch between them from one semester to the next. The T.A.

usually teaches recitation or lab classes (and the occasional lecture), grades papers, and helps create exams and homework assignments. The R.A. is paid to do research on a funded project. If your thesis is related to this research, you get paid to do work that can help you directly with getting through the program.

Graduate School - Survival

In the non-medical STEM fields, it is advantageous to lay the ground work for getting accepted to graduate school and to hit the ground running with a ready to go research project and willing advisor. If your university offers graduate degrees with research fields you like, then it is easier to stay within that campus than to apply to a completely different one. However, I have heard it said that if you go into academia, some employers prefer you to have attended more than one school for the B.S., M.S., and Ph.D. You can check with your professors to see if that applies to your field of study.

Laying the groundwork is simply a matter of showing your worth to a would-be advisor. Your best chance of getting into a graduate program is having a professor willing to sponsor you. The best way to show your worth, besides getting decent grades, is to join a university research lab during your undergraduate program. This gives you exposure to the kinds of work you will do and gives the professors in the lab an idea of how dedicated you are and how quickly you can learn. In addition, you may be able to get started on your research project and determine which professors would be the best fit for you as committee members.

The job at the lab may not pay anything, but it is a good investment in your future if you can pull it off. Talk to your professors about possible opportunities, either to work in a lab, or if that isn't possible, to help with classes they teach. Also consider getting involved with the cooperative education program. The experience is a huge plus for any future employer, including a prospective advisor. It is optimal to start laying the groundwork for graduate school in your sophomore or junior year.

If you are returning to school after some time in industry, your work experience and maturity can be an asset. Figure out which professors are working in your field of interest by reading their profiles on the university website, then set up a face to face interview to discuss your chances of acceptance.

Once you get in, the tools of survival are much like that for undergraduate programs. There are a few differences, though. It is my opinion that the undergraduate degree is the hardest one you'll earn. In the graduate program, professors take you more seriously and are even more interested in your success. You'll probably notice they are more helpful even as you get to your junior and senior years in the B.S. program.

Another thing that makes graduate school easier is that you only have to take 1 – 3 classes at a time, and they are directly related to your major. In undergrad, you have to take a number of electives that may or may not interest you, and within each major there are often specialties that will encompass much of your course load. For example, in electrical engineering, there are electro-magnetic waves, power systems, networks, electronics, and computer science, each of which requires 2-4 courses. In graduate school you pick your key specialty, and perhaps a secondary one, which dictates your coursework.

Don't get me wrong, graduate school is hard, and I don't mean to make light of the workload with advanced classes, original research, and an assistantship. However, with an advisor's support and guidance, a decent paying half-time job, and a greatly reduced course load, you have much more flexibility to meet all of the demands.

Chapter 6: Women & STEM

There has been substantial growth in women's participation in STEM careers in the last decades [1,2]. Unfortunately, the higher paying fields of engineering, computer science, and physics are still suffering an underrepresentation of women [3,4].

> *Although more women than men are enrolled in college within the Unites States, women remain underrepresented in critical areas of study such as science, technology, engineering, and mathematics (STEM). This is particularly concerning given that STEM fields of study are vital to the economic growth and workforce development within the United States (Commission on Professionals in Science and Technology, 2006; National Science Board, 2006) [4].*

Having more women in these fields not only improves innovation; the work environment benefits, as well. For example, now that women have been impacting STEM communities more, the culture of the workplace is changing. Obviously things like sexual harassment and discrimination have fallen sharply, but there are also other major impacts. Several studies have shown that women's more inclusive management style, soliciting employee input before rendering final decisions for example, is preferred over the previous standards by large margins [5]. Many companies now teach these styles as part of their management training processes. In addition, things like child-care, job-sharing, and telecommuting were championed by many women in large corporations seeking to balance work with other responsibilities [5]. It makes one wonder how much better off we'd be with more diversity at the office.

NOW 2 kNOW™ STEM-ing the Tide

Chapter 6: Women & STEM

Statistics

So, let's take stock of where we are with women participation in STEM. Figure 6-1 shows that the ratio of women to men in the U.S. population is fairly evenly distributed [6], yet women earn more Bachelor of Science degrees by a wide margin [7]. This is good news since B.S. graduates enjoy higher pay and less unemployment than those with a less advanced degree. But, not all majors are created equal as discussed earlier in this book.

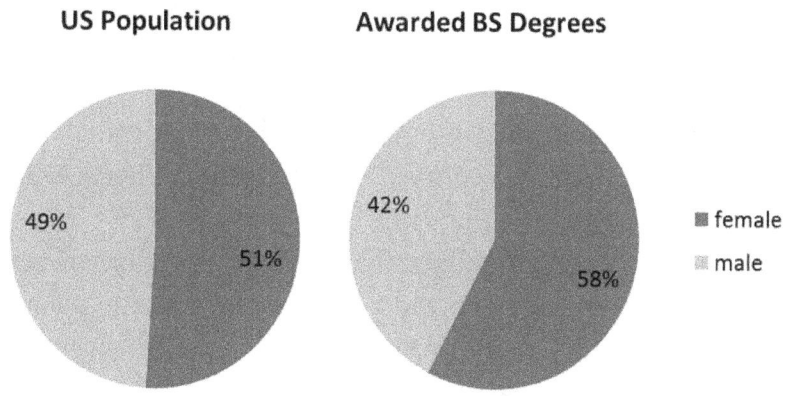

Figure 6-1: 2010 distribution of U.S. population [6] and 2008 BS degrees [7] by gender.

Figure 6-2 shows that the number of women achieving a B.S. in non-health care majors is substantially lower, and there is a great underrepresentation of female B.S. recipients in engineering and computer science [3].

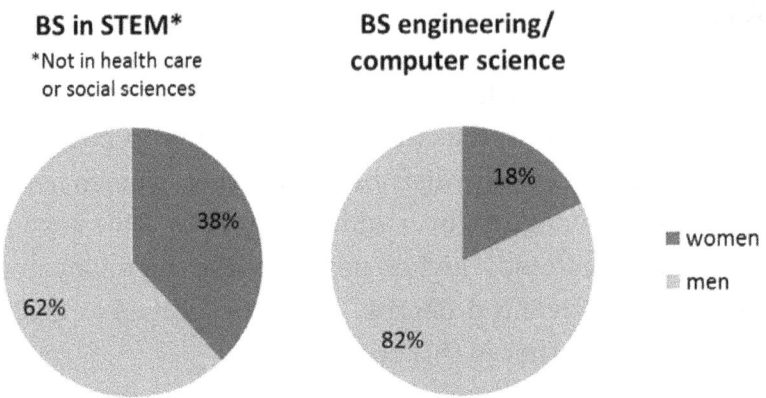

Figure 6-2: 2008 distribution of BS degrees by major and gender [3].

The lack of women attaining these degrees translates into underrepresentation in the workforce, as expected. Figure 6-3 shows the breakdown of gender composition for selected STEM careers [8]. Numbers shown in grey highlight where the percentage of males or females is less than 10% of their proportion in the overall U.S. population. As can be seen, there are a plethora of careers where female representation is vastly lower than their representation in the population at large. This translates into lower pay potentials for women versus men, a situation I find hard to accept.

	Male	Female
% Population	49.2	50.8
% of Employed 16yrs/older	52.8	47.2
Accountant	40	60
Aerospace Engineer	89	11
Architect	76	24
Biological Scientist	54	46
Chemical Engineer	83	17
Chemist/Material Scientist	66	34
Civil Engineer	90	10
Computer HW Engineer	90	10
Computer Programmer	78	22
Computer SW Engineer	79	21
Financial Analyst	64	36
Industrial Engineer	80	20
Mechanical Engineer	93	7
Pharmacist	47	53
Physician/Surgeon	68	32
Registered Nurse	9	91
Veterinarian	44	56

Figure 6-3: 2010 Data from U.S. Census Bureau and U.S. Bureau of Labor Statistics showing gender composition of selected STEM careers [8].

Furthermore, if you are a female minority, you are susceptible to the "double bind" of underrepresentation from gender and ethnicity, with ethnicity effects trumping gender effects [2,3]. Figure 6-4 shows the breakdown of non-health care STEM degrees awarded to women of various backgrounds [3].

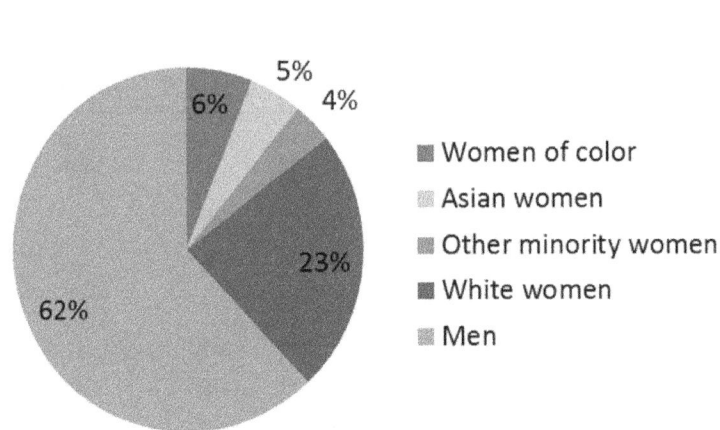

Figure 6-4: 2008 distribution of BS STEM degrees by ethnicity and gender [3].

As a result of the current state of STEM participation by women, many studies have been conducted to understand why the gap persists despite the improvement seen in last decades. Possible causes can be broken down in the following categories, each of which is addressed in the rest of this chapter:

- They don't want to (lack of interest)
- They can't (lack of ability)
- Someone is stopping them (discrimination)
- Other

Interest

It would appear that women tend to have less interest in the physical sciences, mathematics, computer and information sciences, and engineering than men. In 2009, 17% of female college freshman expressed interest in these fields as compared to 32% of males [9]. If bachelor degree majors are an indication of interest, the following chart clearly underlines this trend [10].

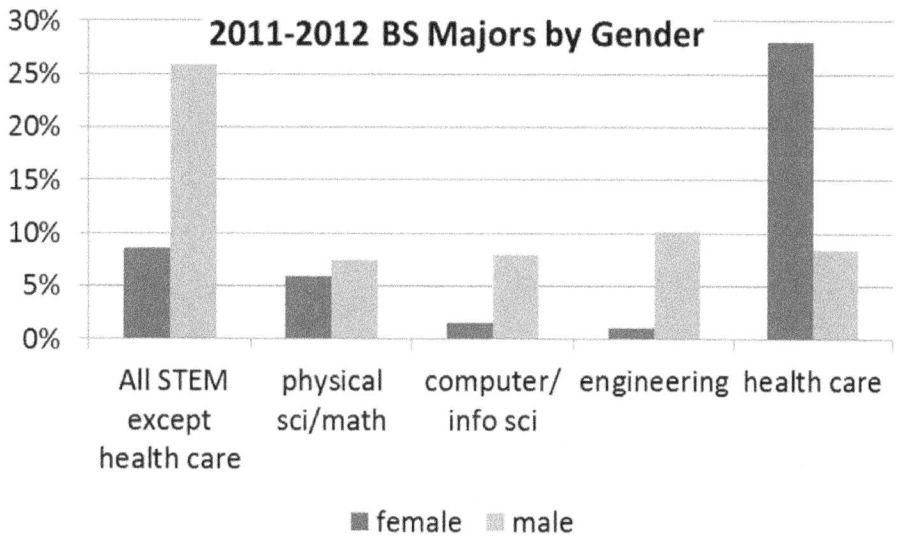

Figure 6-5: 2011-12 major distribution of BS students by gender [10].

Only 8.6% of women pursuing baccalaureates in the 2011-12 school year majored in non-health related STEM subjects as opposed to 25.8% of men [10]. However, the trend is almost completely reversed in health care majors (28% of women, 8.4% of men) [10]. I group health care studies with STEM because they are all about science, and many medical schools want applicants who have succeeded in calculus, computer science, and statistics. Under this broader definition, women received 52% of all BS degrees in STEM in 2010 [11]. Why all of the fuss then about underrepresentation?

The next figure shows the distribution by hourly wages for some of the job groups in the STEM discipline [12]. Physical science data were not separate from social science data, so they were not included.

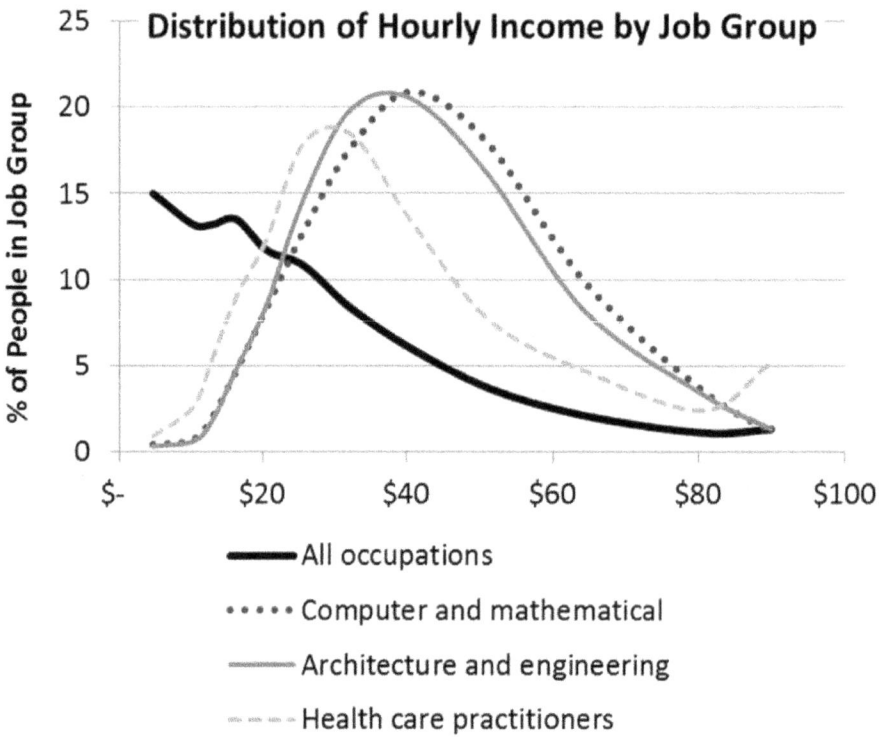

Figure 6-6: May 2013 income distribution by job group [12]

Notice how the curve for all occupations is heavily weighted to the low end owing to the many people in non-STEM careers. Notice, too, that the median health care practitioner makes at least $10 less per hour than the computer scientist or engineer. That adds up to over $20,000 per year! Unless you are going all the way to an M.D. (the uptick at the end of the health care practitioner curve), then you may be missing out on some earning potential.

In fact, according to Figure 6-3, women are underrepresented in the physician/surgeon category [8]. That is why people are trying to encourage more women to participate in other STEM professions. The U.S. Department of Labor stated in 2010 that engineers are among the highest paid of all B.S. graduates fresh out of a four year program [13]. If an engineering discipline interests you, it's worth considering the high payout for only four years of study.

There is a theory that women prefer to pursue careers that they perceive as directly impacting real life situations and people [9]. The data on 2011-12 majors seems to support this theory. While it is true that health care impacts people very directly, so do the other sciences. Exploring space, connecting people with new technology, building infrastructure, and creating new foods and materials are very impactful.

It's also possible that the lack of interest seen to date has been about exposure. Not everyone knows what an engineer or a computer scientist or a financial analyst does. Young males have historically been more encouraged to enter such fields. With recent outreach programs and concerted efforts, women's awareness of these occupations and therefore enrollment in STEM majors has increased over the last decades [1,2].

The Department of Defense has published a website at www.myfuture.com that gives detailed information about any career you type in. But, when searching for potential careers, it is nice to have a collection of choices with similar facts about each. The *NOW 2 kNOW™ High-Paying Careers in STEM* book features over 80 STEM careers with $55,000+ per year median compensation. Each career is described with daily tasks, work environment, education requirements, salary ranges, and projected job growth. Once you narrow down your choices with this or another source, the DoD website can fill in additional information.

Ability

Okay, hold your nose, because here come some statistics that can be hard to swallow. The average 2011 score on the SAT Math section (SATM) was 500 for women and 531 for men [11]. In addition, the following two charts show a noticeable difference in the scores of 12th graders taking the National Assessment of Educational Progress (NAEP) tests in math and science in 2009.

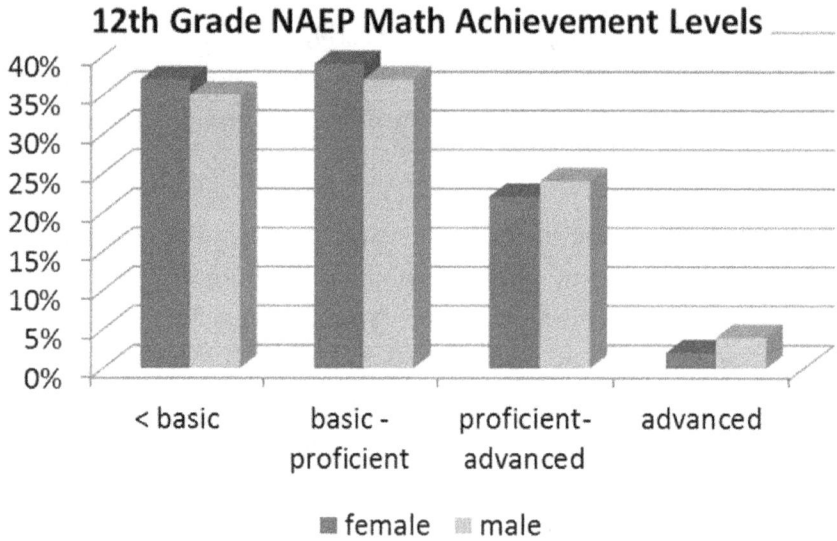

Figure 6-7: 2009 12th Grade NAEP math achievement levels by gender [11].

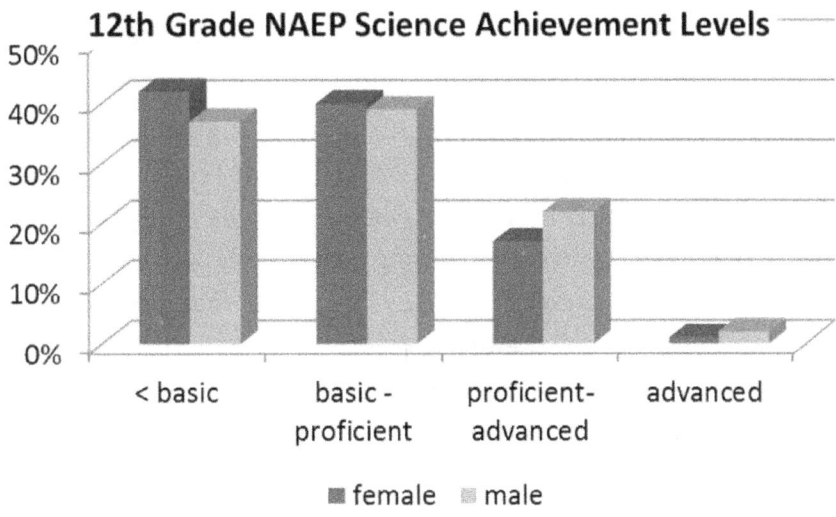

Figure 6-8: 2009 12th Grade NAEP math achievement levels by gender [11].

On the other hand, we have these data [14]:

- Girls take more math and science classes in K-12 than boys, the exception being physics.
- Girls consistently get better grades than boys across all subjects in high school and college.

The above data suggest that there's a difference between classroom performance and standardized test performance. There are several theories on the matter. One theory is that boys have a speed advantage over girls owing to "culture conflict" [2]. Culture conflict poses that boys are low-context, paradigmatic thinkers that deal in objectivity and logic; girls are high-context, narrative thinkers that work on more subtle cues and interconnections. Standardized tests are presented in the low-context, paradigmatic style, and perhaps girls lose time on interpreting the questions into their own way of processing information [2].

Another speed advantage may be found in the idea that boys are more apt to be risk takers, so they are more comfortable with guessing answers than are girls [2]. Similarly, they are also more prone to use unconventional solving techniques such as working backwards from the answers given in multiple choice tests [2]. It should be pointed out that speed in math and science is not necessarily a desired trait of the more complex problem solving required in higher level coursework or career level challenges [2]. But, these standardized tests are a gateway to college and careers, so it would be nice if we knew how to better compete as women.

A very strong predictor of how well a student will do on such tests is spatial reasoning, specifically the ability to conceptualize object rotations [2,14]. For example, if given a die as in the top of Figure 6-9, can you predict the three rotations shown below it (with a single dot placed on the unknown side)? Since girls tend to have more developed left brains for language, and boys tend to have more developed right brains for abstraction, there used to be an expectation that boys would be better at spatial reasoning [14,15].

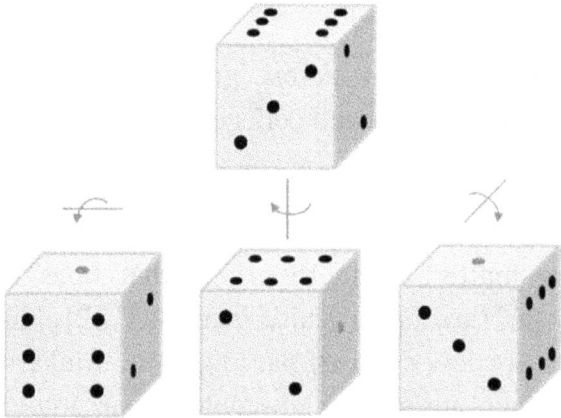

Figure 6-9: Die rotation where the new side that comes into view gets a single dot.

The good news is that we now know spatial reasoning can be learned. The reason boys are so good at it can be attributed to the types of playtime activities they enjoyed as kids like Lego™ construction, sports, and video games [14]. Girls who also engaged in such activities performed just as well as their male counterparts [14]. When asked to play hours of video games, spatial reasoning scores increased among all tested groups regardless of age or gender [14].

Finally, there is "stereotype threat" and the ideas of self-confidence and test anxiety [2,14]. Stereotype threat describes the impact on a person's performance when confronted with an expectation or stereotype. In 1998, the University of Michigan conducted a social experiment where they presented a difficult math test (questions taken from the GRE) to undergraduate students who normally did well in math [14]. Two groups were formed, each with women and men, but one group was told before the exam that there was no expected gender difference in test performance. The other group was told the opposite. The following figure shows how reminding students of the stereotype greatly reduced the performance of women, and also greatly improved the performance of men [14].

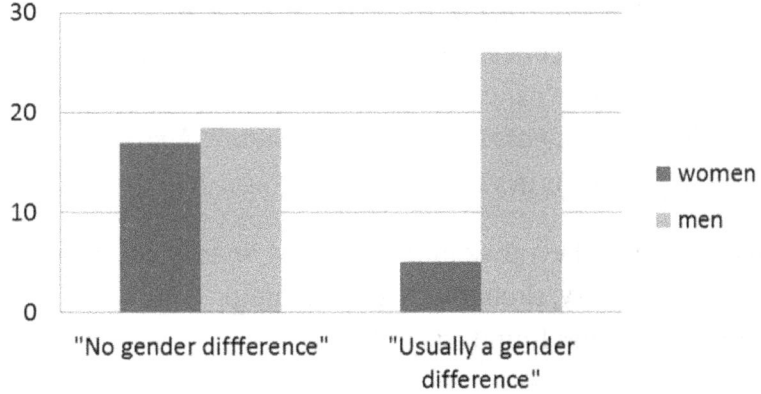

Figure 6-10: Stereotype threat math test experiment results [14].

Stereotype threat seems to affect all people for whom a negative stereotype exists. As examples, white males were negatively affected by stereotype threat when performing against Asian males on math tests, against black men in sports, and against women in social sensitivity assessments [14]. Couple stereotype threat with a pension for low self-confidence and test anxiety [2,14], and it's no wonder that women can underperform their actual ability on standardized tests.

Discrimination

The Huffington Post published an article in 2014 with the results of a HuffPost Science survey [16]. Women were asked via the anonymous Whisper app if they had been discouraged in STEM because of their gender, and 24 of their disheartening comments are posted at the end of the article. Though this isn't a scientific study, and I can tell you that I did not encounter overt sexism in my pursuit of STEM, it would be irresponsible not to acknowledge that someone on your path may tell you that STEM isn't for girls. See it as bullshit and move on.

Some of the comments can be painful (I have experienced sexism in other areas in life), and I don't mean to detract from that. But, there will always be someone trying to stand in your way, whether it's a chauvinist, a weed-out course, an impossible to understand instructor, etc. In such circumstances, you have to fight for what you want. Too few role models, lack of parental encouragement? Again, it's up to you to decide what you want in your life and to go get it.

When discrimination becomes more than just snarky comments and denies you opportunity, then it's time to get help. A study in 2004-05 among women in STEM found the following [9]:

- Almost one third of women felt they were treated differently by professors.
- Twenty percent of women were uncomfortable asking questions in class.
- Almost one fourth of women were uncomfortable seeking help from professors after class.

If your professor truly is a jerk, grading you differently, excluding you, and discouraging you from understanding the material, then go to the next level. The department chair or even the dean will typically be anxious about anyone discouraging women or minorities in STEM. They may be able to help you confront the professor or find another less direct but effective solution. There are also likely to be other campus resources and organizations that will be happy to help.

Other

One other trend that came out in the literature points to why fewer women get into or stay in engineering, computer science, or physics. The phrase "chilly climate" is used by some to characterize the competitive and aloof college environment in STEM [9]. Classrooms can be large, especially in freshman year, which generally don't allow much in the way of classroom participation. With hundreds of students in a class, the professor may not have a very good open door policy. The grading is done "on a curve", or relative to other students, which means there are only so many A's, B's, etc. awarded. Some curves are constructed so that someone has to fail. Such grading practices tend to pit students against each other. And, group activities in the lab or classroom can become opportunities to isolate or exclude women, especially minority women.

Many affordable colleges with STEM degrees are very large. One suggestion to ease into such an environment is to consider starting off at a community college [17]. The classes are smaller encouraging more student participation, and by the time you enter your junior year at a university, the class sizes have decreased significantly.

No matter where you go to school, engaging in other student activities on your campus will help ease feelings of isolation and exclusion [3]. Check out your university's clubs and organizations and get involved. You will likely find lots of students willing to share similar stories and offer support. There are far more people out there willing to help you than to drag you down.

References

[1] Gayles, Joy Gaston. "Editor's Notes," *Attracting and Retaining Women in STEM*. No. 152, Wiley Periodicals, Inc., Winter 2011.

[2] Gallager, Ann M. & Kaufman, James C., ed. *Gender Differences in Mathematics: An Integrative Psychological Approach*. Cambridge University Press, 2005.

[3] Johnson, Dawn R. "Women of Color in Science, Technology, Engineering, and Mathematics (STEM)," *Attracting and Retaining Women in STEM*. No. 152, Wiley Periodicals, Inc., Winter 2011.

[4] Gayles, Joy Gaston & Ampaw, Frim D. "Gender Matters: An Examination of Differential Effects of the College Experience on Degree Attainment in STEM," *Attracting and Retaining Women in STEM*. No. 152, Wiley Periodicals, Inc., Winter 2011.

[5]   O'Brien, Virginia. *Success on Our Own Terms: Tales of Extraordinary, Ordinary Business Women.* John Wiley & Sons, Inc., 1998.

{6}   U.S. Census Bureau. Data minded from the United States Census 2010: http://www.census.gov/2010census/data/.

[7]   U.S. Department of Education. *Today's Baccalaureate: The Fields and Courses that 2007-08 Bachelor's Degree Recipients Studied.* National Center for Education Statistics, NCES 2013-755, May 2013: http://nces.ed.gov/pubs2013/2013755.pdf.

[8]   U.S. Department of Labor. *Household Data Annual Averages.* U.S. Bureau of Labor Statistics, 2010 Annual Averages: http://www.bls.gov/cps/aa2010/cpsaat11.pdf.

[9]   Shapiro, Casey A. & Sax, Linda J. "Major Selection and Persistence for Women in STEM," *Attracting and Retaining Women in STEM.* No. 152, Wiley Periodicals, Inc., Winter 2011.

[10] U.S. Department of Education. *Profile of Undergraduate Students: 2011-12.* National Center for Education Statistics, NCES 2015-167, October 2014: http://nces.ed.gov/pubs2015/2015167.pdf.

[11] U.S. Department of Education. *Higher Education: Gaps in Access and Persistence Study.* Institute of Educational Sciences & National Center for Education Statistics, NCES 2012-046, August 2012: http://nces.ed.gov/pubs2012/2012046.pdf.

[12] U.S. Department of Labor. *Occupational Employment Statistics.* U.S. Bureau of Labor Statistics, May 2013: http://www.bls.gov/oes/2013/may/distribution.htm.

[13] U.S. Department of Labor. *Occupational Outlook Handbook: 2010-2011 Edition.* 2010.

[14]   Eliot, Lise. *Pink Brain, Blue Brain: How Small Differences Grow Into Troublesome Gaps – and What We Can Do About It.* First Mariner Books, 2010.

[15]   Gurian, Michael & Stevens, Kathy. *Boys & Girls Learn Differently!: A guide for Teachers and Parents.* Jossey-Bass, 2011.

[16]   Cooper-White, Macrina. "Read the Nasty Comments Women in Science Deal With Daily," *HuffPost Science.* The Huffington Post, February 2, 2015: http://www.huffingtonpost.com/2014/09/25/women-in-stem-stories-whisper_n_5844678.html.

[17]   Jackson, Dimitra Lynette & Laanan, Frankie Santos. "The Role of Community Colleges in Educating Women in Science and Engineering," *Attracting and Retaining Women in STEM.* No. 152, Wiley Periodicals, Inc., Winter 2011.

Chapter 7: Minorities & STEM

There is a common preconception that STEM careers are reserved for white males only. The fact is that women and minorities are just as capable as white males when it comes to math and science. And, producing adequate numbers of qualified STEM graduates is considered a national priority [1]:

> *Rising concerns about the ability of the United States to compete in the global economy have led to numerous calls for national efforts to increase the number and diversity of students pursuing degrees and careers in STEM fields (National Academy of Science 2005; National Governors Association 2007; National Research Council 2012; National Science Board 2007).*

Believe it or not, you are missed! Corporations and universities are vying to recruit minorities as quickly as they can. They know that diversity in perspective stimulates the creative process, leads to better innovation, and brings a breath of fresh air to established regimes. Not only does lack of diversity cause technical advancements to suffer, but the workplace suffers, as well.

Statistics

In this book, I will be using the terms white, black, Hispanic, and Asian to refer to groups of people with similar physical and/or cultural characteristics. I believe these are the broadest terms that capture people's various races and origins, and they are the terms used by the governmental statistical authorities from which the following data are pulled. People who identify with multiple races or who are from Native American, Hawaiian, or Alaskan cultures are grouped into the "other" category. I apologize now if any terminology used here is found to be lacking. Offense is definitely not intended.

Unlike the near 50/50 distribution of women and men in the U.S., the ethnic make-up of the overall population is important to put other statistics in proper perspective. For example, it's unrealistic to expect a group comprising 10% of the population to hold 50% of the B.S. degrees. As Figure 7-1 shows, there is a disturbing trend in B.S. degrees compared with the U.S. composition by ethnicity [2,3].

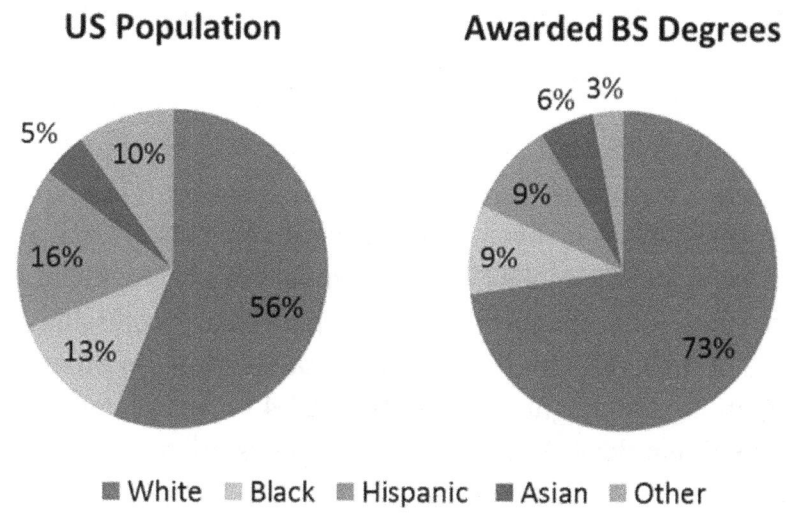

Figure 7-1: 2010 distribution of U.S. population [2] and 2008 BS degrees [3] by ethnicity. To use the key, start at the top and follow clockwise around.

Furthermore, the trend is exacerbated when looking at B.S. and Ph.D. degrees awarded in STEM in 2010. As Figure 7-2 shows, Asians and whites are ensuring their place in STEM fields whereas blacks and Hispanics are sorely underrepresented [4].

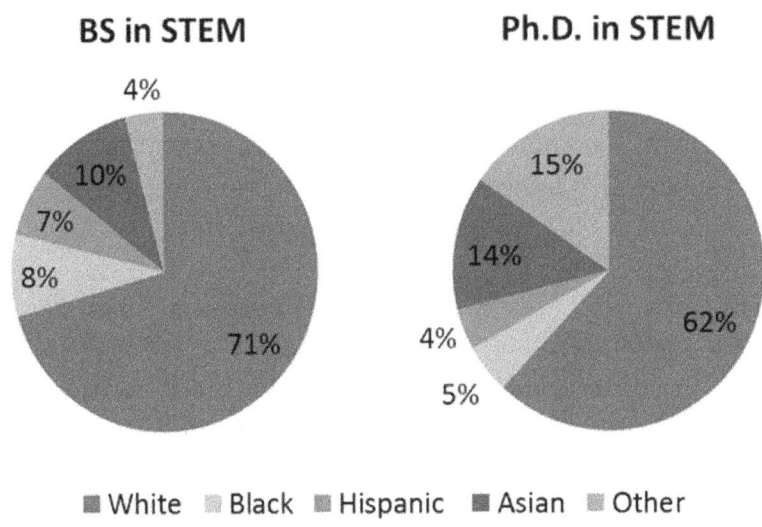

Figure 7-2: 2010 distribution of BS and Ph.D. degrees in STEM by ethnicity [4].

And, in terms of the high paying careers such degrees should secure, the trend continues. Figure 7-3 shows the marked underrepresentation of black and Hispanics in most if not all of a selected group of STEM jobs [5]. The numbers in grey highlight where the percentage of a group occupying a particular profession is less than 10% of their ratio in the overall U.S. population. In other words, an occupation is highlighted if less than 11.4% of that field employs blacks, 4.3% employs Asians, 14.7% employs Hispanics, or 59.7% employs whites or other races.

	White/Other	Black	Asian	Hispanic
% Population	66.3	12.6	4.8	16.3
% of Employed 16yrs/older	70.1	10.8	4.8	14.3
Accountant	76	9	9	6
Aerospace Engineer	85	7	4	4
Architect	88	2	2	8
Biological Scientist	76	8	10	6
Chemical Engineer	84	3	12	1
Chemist/Material Scientist	68	10	18	4
Civil Engineer	79	5	9	7
Computer HW Engineer	63	3	27	7
Computer Programmer	76	5	12	7
Computer SW Engineer	63	5	28	4
Financial Analyst	78	12	7	3
Industrial Engineer	77	5	10	8
Mechanical Engineer	82	3	11	4
Pharmacist	76	5	15	4
Physician/Surgeon	71	6	16	7
Registered Nurse	75	12	8	5
Veterinarian	91	3	2	4

Figure 7-3: 2010 Data from U.S. Census Bureau and U.S. Bureau of Labor Statistics showing ethnic composition of selected STEM careers [5].

As I look at this chart, I see a big red flag on social equality. Why aren't there more blacks and Hispanics in these high-paying professions? Where do we lose people in the pipeline to such in-demand careers? As we'll see, the underlying causes share many similarities to the case of female underrepresentation in STEM, but there are some very notable differences.

Possible causes can be broken down in the following categories, each of which is addressed in the rest of this chapter:

- They don't want to (lack of interest)
- They can't (lack of ability)
- Someone is stopping them (discrimination)
- Other

Interest

Unlike in the case of women, blacks and Hispanics indeed have a very strong interest in STEM careers. Figure 7-4 shows the average of four studies presented in a 2010 briefing to the U.S. Commission on Civil Rights [6]. In these studies, black and Hispanic high school students showed slightly more interest than whites in pursuing STEM majors in college.

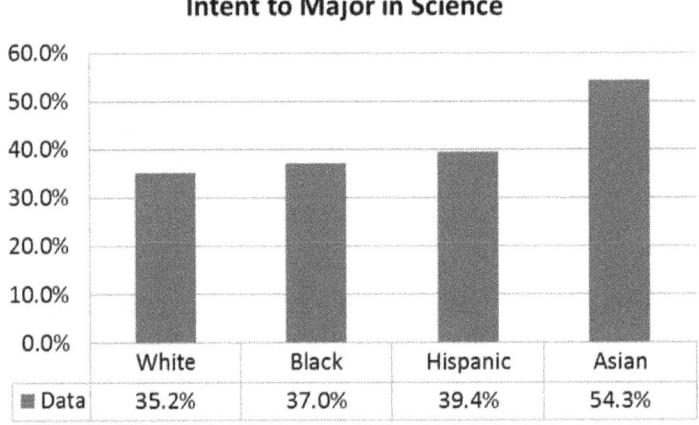

Figure 7-4: Interest expressed of high school seniors to major in science by ethnicity as averaged over four studies presented to the 2010 U.S. Commission on Civel Rights [6].

Looking at the distribution of each group's majors in the 2011-2012 college school year, shown in Figure 7-5, we see comparable intent between whites, blacks, and Hispanics to pursue STEM [7]. According to these numbers, 36% of white students, 34% of black students, 34% of Hispanic students, and 42% of Asian students majored in STEM (including health care). Clearly, lack of interest is not the underlying cause of underrepresentation.

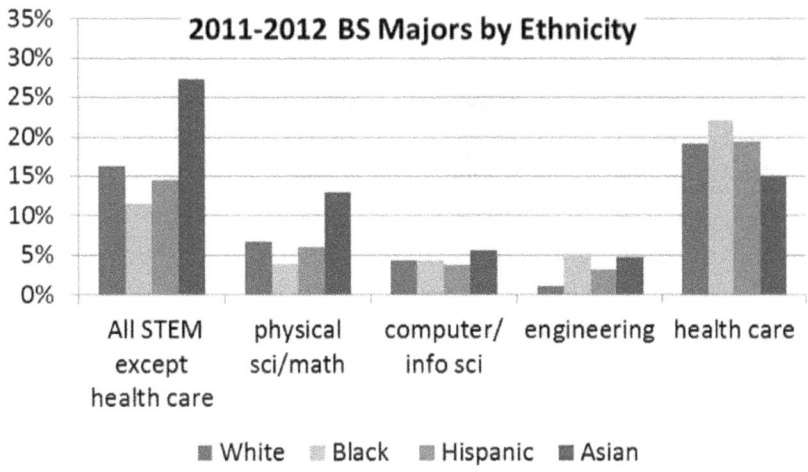

Figure 7-5: 2011-12 major distribution of BS students by ethnicity [7].

Ability

We start with some bad news, but don't take it at face value as there's more here than meets the eye. Figure 7-6 shows the average SAT math (SATM) scores in 2011 as broken down by ethnicity [4]. With an 800 being a perfect score, no one group is doing exceptionally well. However, it is clear that scores are significantly highest for Asians and significantly lower for blacks and Hispanics. The SAT is a very high stakes exam, so even if you don't agree that the test is an indication of future college or career achievement, it will impact your chances of getting into college to have a chance at future success.

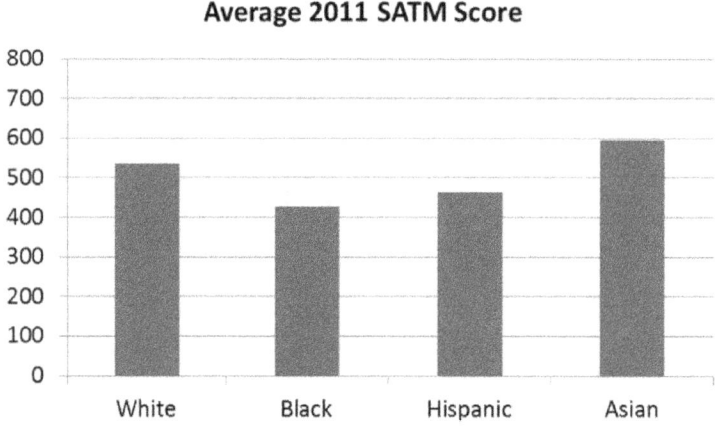

Figure 7-6: 2011 SATM scores by ethnicity [4].

Furthermore, as we did in the chapter on women, we can look at the breakdown of 12th grade students taking the National Assessment of Educational Progress (NAEP) tests in math and science. In Figure 7-7, the math results show the largest percentage of white students in the basic to proficient achievement level, Asian students have highest representation in the proficient to advanced achievement level, and the highest percentage of black and Hispanic students were at the less than basic level [4]. A similar trend occurs on the NAEP science proficiency test, shown in Figure 7-8, except that the Asian profile matches that of the whites [4]. With only four levels to group students, this isn't exactly a fine measurement; however it does clearly show a problem. Let's dig a little deeper into some underlying causes.

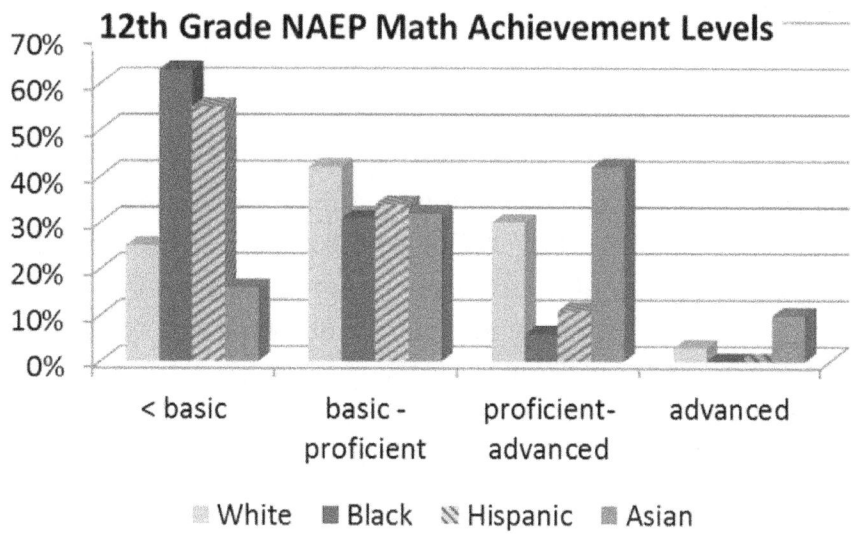

Figure 7-7: 2009 12th Grade NAEP math achievement levels by gender [4].

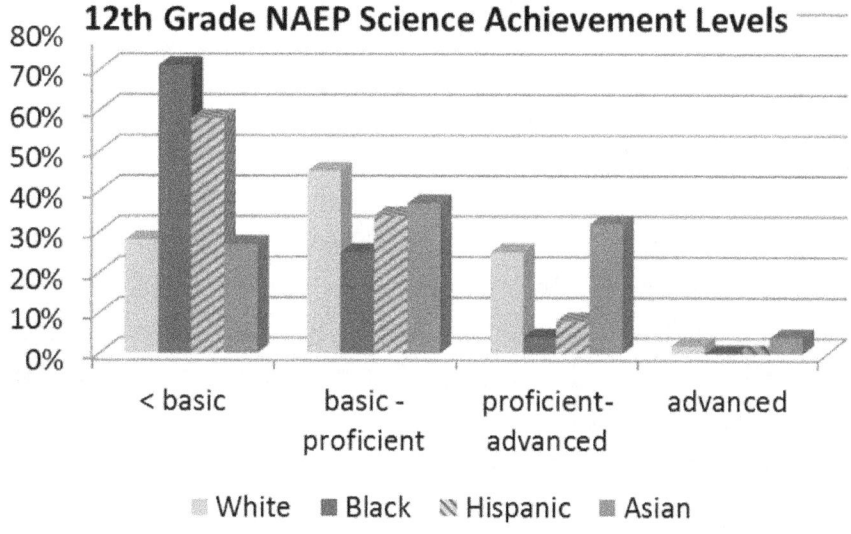

Figure 7-8: 2009 12th Grade NAEP math achievement levels by gender [4].

As was described in the corresponding Ability section of Chapter 6 regarding women in STEM, factors such as "stereotype threat" and "culture conflict" can strongly influence results [8,9].

Stereotype threat describes the impact on a person's performance when confronted with an expectation or stereotype. Chapter 6 shows an example of how presenting students with gender stereotypes prior to math tests greatly affected results (see Figure 6-10). Similar findings have been shown with ethnic stereotypes in various test scenarios [8,9]. As math is stereotypically the domain of white or Asian males, some lack of self-confidence could affect results. It is interesting to note that black females tend to outperform black males on math tests, the opposite being true for Hispanics [9].

In addition, thinking styles can vary among ethnic groups leading to a situation called "culture conflict" where classes are conducted in one style while students learn in an alternate style. The analytical style of the classroom may not effectively meet the relational learning style held by some. The relational style of learning is creative and flexible versus the rigid and rule-driven analytical style of most schools [10].

But, let's not forget the elephant in the room - poverty. Figure 7-9 shows median household income by ethnicity from 1967-2013 [11]. There has been a very consistent discrepancy in wages throughout this history indicating poor wages for blacks and Hispanics, better wages for whites, and the best wages for Asians. Coupled with other data in this book, I would argue that a part of this discrepancy is due to choice of occupation. It is my opinion, and the reason I wrote this book, that one way to have control over breaking out of the averages is to choose and prepare for high paying careers, like those in STEM.

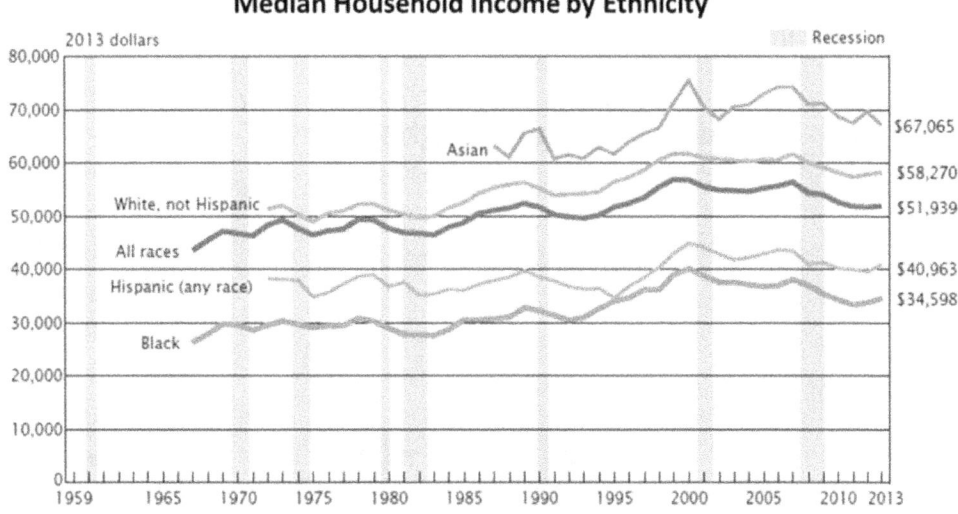

Figure 7-9: Median income by ethnicity from 1967-2013, photograph [11].

As a note, there was a widely circulated statistic presented at the end of 2014 that showed the median white household net worth was $142,000 and that for black households was $11,000 [12]. Net worth involves income as well as ownership of things such as stocks, houses, heirlooms, etc. This book is intended to focus on what an individual can do in terms of income to better their status. Investment and inheritance are topics for a different title, but the statistic is mentioned here to avoid confusion.

There is definitely an income (and wealth) divide among ethnicities. Poor parents are likely working long hours, some also struggle with the language, and this makes it hard for them to help their kids with schoolwork. Unfortunately, the income inequality is also passed to children in the types of schools they attend. Figure 7-10 shows that white and Asian children attend low poverty K-12 schools at about the same rate as blacks and Hispanics attend high poverty schools [4].

Low and high poverty schools are labeled by the percentage of kids eligible for low cost or free lunch programs.

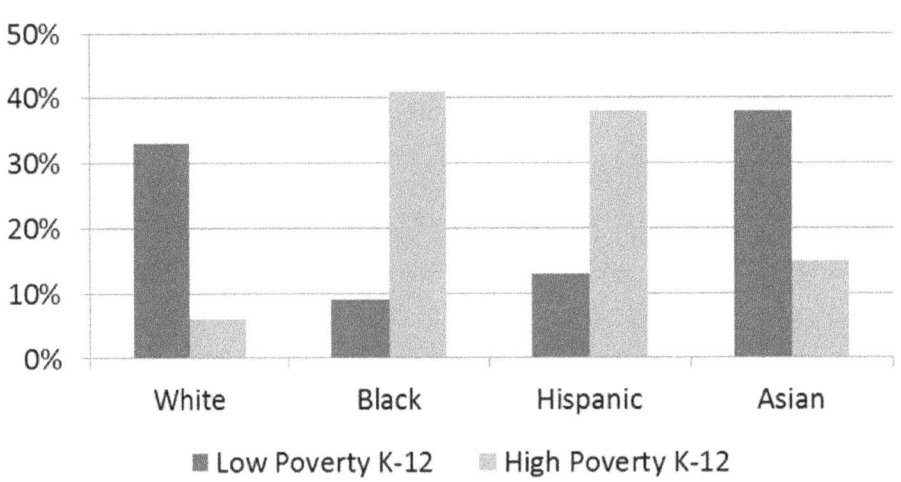

Figure 7-10: 2010-11 students in low poverty (<25% of kids eligible for low priced lunch program) and high poverty (>75% of kids eligible for low priced lunch program) public K-12 schools [4].

At least 44% of high poverty schools have math instructors with no math certification [6]. And, studies have shown that 50-75% of high poverty school teachers cannot answer basic math questions [6]. Math is a cumulative subject with each year based on the prior year. If you get crippled with a poor foundation, you stagnate for the rest of your education. To paraphrase one leading researcher on the topic: higher math is easy unless you haven't learned the prior courses, yet [6]. It seems clear to me that standardized tests do not tell the whole story of potential and ability. One reason that I've written the NOW 2 kNOW™ math series is to provide an affordable way to get fast instruction with tons of examples so you can catch up on these subjects at your own pace.

Discrimination

In the Findings and Recommendations section of the 2010 Briefing to the U.S. Commission on Civil Rights, the following was published regarding blacks and Hispanics who chose not to pursue STEM [6]:

> *Data presented to the Commission indicated that racial or ethnic discrimination in college was not a substantial factor in black and Hispanic college students' disproportionate attrition from STEM majors. The evidence showed that when black and white students have the same academic index scores, black students are more likely than white students to receive a STEM degree. [Approved 4-0-3]*

The bracketed "Approval 4-0-3" means that when the finding was brought to a vote, four were in favor, none were against, and three abstained.

Okay, let's assume there is no one at the "gates to college" wielding a sword shouting, "None of ye of black or Hispanic ancestry may enter yon!" But, most of us know that discrimination is still around, intentional or otherwise.

Studies from 2005-2009 revealed that minorities in STEM majors felt isolated, ignored, or worse [13]. In particular, avoidance by students when choosing groups for lab or class assignments, discouragement by faculty, lack of role models, and exclusion from academic or research opportunities were reported [13]. In a 2010 survey of minority chemists and chemical engineers, nearly 40% of participants said they experienced some discouragement along the way, mostly from college professors [14]. Women of color bear the brunt of these appalling affronts as a result of the "double bind," coined in 1976 to refer to shouldering the struggles of both female and minority prejudices [13].

Some recommendations for dealing with such treatment have been offered in the literature. These include getting involved in other activities at your college to offset the isolation or attending colleges with more minority representation [13]. No matter the course you choose, it's important to know going in what you may face, but please don't let a few dissenting opinions stand in the way of your much deserved future.

Other

The lack of quality training from high poverty K-12 schools is one of the biggest issues facing minority STEM hopefuls, as alluded to in the quote of the prior section [6]. When equally matched in preparation, minority students are at least as likely to succeed in their STEM careers as whites [6]. Unfortunately, our high poverty schools are not providing students with such an opportunity. In fact, 2011-12 college students in the lowest income bracket were 50% more likely to take a remedial math class than those in the highest income bracket [7].

The term "mismatch" is used to describe the situation where a student is significantly more advanced or significantly less advanced than the average student in his or her classroom. In either case, the mismatched student becomes disengaged either from boredom or feeling overwhelmed with the pace of the material [6]. As such, minority college freshmen from a high poverty K-12 background may find themselves severely disadvantaged in a STEM class in a top tier university.

The effects of mismatch are so significant that they trump gender and other ethnic barriers to STEM careers [6].

Affirmative action started off as a well-intentioned and much needed policy in many aspects of America. Today, many top tier universities recruit students from underrepresented minority groups independent of their academic preparation [6]. This causes a cascade effect where lower tier schools implement similar policies, but with their qualified students accepted elsewhere they recruit other students with relatively deficient academic preparation [6]. The result is a much higher dropout rate in STEM for underrepresented minorities affected by mismatch [6]. They get the great news that they've been accepted to a good school only to find themselves failing out not long after. They seem doomed before they even try.

There were two suggestions put forth in the 2010 briefing to the U.S. Commission on Civil Rights regarding mismatch and STEM attrition for minorities. One suggestion was for a high poverty student to attend a lower tier institution [6]. The thought was that it would be better to complete a less prestigious degree than to fail out altogether. Though the sentiment is intended to be helpful, it is not the best choice in my opinion. The highest paid positions in academia, for example, would not consider a student from anything but a top research university [6].

The other suggestion presented was that prospective students accept their offer of admission but [6]:

- Determine their relative class status;
- Ask what tools the university is offering to support them.

Many students accepted to a top tier university may be receiving good grades from their current school and not realize the academic deficit that exists between them and other would-be peer students. Good grades don't indicate the quality of the K-12 education given. A comparison of SATM scores can help determine if mismatch exists. Remember, you are looking at a *significant* gap between your score and that of the average accepted student. Minor gaps could be attributed to any number of unrelated issues.

Some schools offer pre-freshman year summer school courses to help students get a better mathematical foundation [6]. Ask if such a program exists or if other mentoring/tutoring opportunities are available. If the school isn't offering an affordable option, look into private tutoring or read on your own.

The good news is that with Latinos expected to reach 25% of the U.S. population in four decades, there is a vast untapped resource for the STEM industries [6]. As a direct result, large companies such as IBM, Exxon Mobil, and Lockheed Martin are developing programs to specifically recruit Hispanics to STEM education and help the high poverty school system [6].

In addition, with access to and preparation for high paying careers being a social equality issue, President Barack Obama issued an executive order in 2012 entitled "White House Initiative on Educational Excellence for African Americans" [15]. The main goal is to address the quality of K-12 education experienced by the majority of black Americans. As stated in Section 1 [15]:

> ...substantial obstacles to equal educational opportunity still remain in America's educational system. African Americans lack equal access to highly effective teachers and principals, safe schools, and challenging college-preparatory classes, and they disproportionately experience school discipline and referrals to special education.

Your road may be more difficult than others, but you are not alone in your struggle.

References

[1]   U.S. Department of Education. *STEM Attrition: College Students' Paths Into and Out of STEM Fields.* Institute of Educational Sciences & National Center for Education Statistics, NCES 2014-001, November 2013: http://nces.ed.gov/pubs2014/2014001rev.pdf.

[2] U.S. Census Bureau. Data minded from the United States Census 2010: http://www.census.gov/2010census/data/.

[3] U.S. Department of Education. *Today's Baccalaureate: The Fields and Courses that 2007-08 Bachelor's Degree Recipients Studied.* National Center for Education Statistics, NCES 2013-755, May 2013: http://nces.ed.gov/pubs2013/2013755.pdf.

[4] U.S. Department of Education. *Higher Education: Gaps in Access and Persistence Study.* Institute of Educational Sciences & National Center for Education Statistics, NCES 2012-046, August 2012: http://nces.ed.gov/pubs2012/2012046.pdf.

[5] U.S. Department of Labor. *Household Data Annual Averages.* U.S. Bureau of Labor Statistics, 2010 Annual Averages: http://www.bls.gov/cps/aa2010/cpsaat11.pdf.

[6] "Encouraging Minority Students to Pursue Science, Technology, Engineering, and Math Careers," *A Briefing Before the United States Commission on Civil Rights Held in Washington, DC.* Approved June 11, 2010.

[7] U.S. Department of Education. *Profile of Undergraduate Students: 2011-12.* National Center for Education Statistics, NCES 2015-167, October 2014: http://nces.ed.gov/pubs2015/2015167.pdf.

[8] Eliot, Lise. *Pink Brain, Blue Brain: How Small Differences Grow Into Troublesome Gaps – and What We Can Do About It.* First Mariner Books, 2010.

[9] Gallager, Ann M. & Kaufman, James C., ed. *Gender Differences in Mathematics: An Integrative Psychological Approach.* Cambridge University Press, 2005.

[10] Hale, Janice E. *Black Children: Their Roots, Culture, and Learning Styles*, Revised Edition. Johns Hopkins University Press, 1986.

[11] DeNavas-Walt, Carmen & Proctor, Bernadette D. "Income and Poverty in the United States: 2013," *Current Population Reports*. U.S. Census Bureau, P60-249, September2014: http://www.census.gov/content/dam/Census/library/publications/2014/demo/p60-249.pdf.

[12] Luhby, Tami. "Whites Get Wealthier, While Blacks and Hispanics Lag Further Behind," *CNNMoney*. New York, Dec 15, 2014: 7:27 AM ET: http://money.cnn.com/2014/12/12/news/economy/wealth-by-race-pew/index.html.

[13] U.S. Department of Labor. *Occupational Outlook Handbook: 2010-2011 Edition*. 2010.

[14] Hernandez, Arelis. "Survey: U.S. Women and Minority Scientists Often Discouraged from Pursuing STEM Careers," *Diverse Issues in Higher Education*. March 23, 2010: http://diverseeducation.com/article/13644.

[15] President Obama, Barack. *Executive Order – White House Initieative on Educational Excellence for African Americans.* The White House, Office of the Press Secretary, July 26, 2012: http://www.whitehouse.gov/the-press-office/2012/07/26/executive-order-white-house-initiative-educational-excellence-african-am.

Chapter 8: Choose a STEM Career

Picking a profession for the rest of your life may seem like a daunting task. It is. However, when you make good money, you get to have interesting mid-career options. You may decide to go into management or stay in the technical arena. You might specialize in an area slightly different than where you started or change gears entirely and go back to school. Or, perhaps you'll even take a sabbatical to travel, do volunteer work, or pursue a special interest.

No matter if you are currently in high school ready to start your adult life or if you're out in the workforce thinking about a change, you are looking for a career that is a good fit. There are so many choices and possibilities, and the task of choosing just one can be overwhelming. The following sections will help you narrow it down. We first ask a few pointed questions to get you thinking then look at three important factors in the choosing process: impact, day to day experiences, and preparation time.

Once you narrow down the field a bit, there are many sources for additional information. The *NOW 2 kNOW™ High-Paying Careers in STEM* book lists over 80 careers that have a median pay of >$55,000 per year and up to four times the average in job growth over the next decade. Each career entry gives you a description of the job, day to day tasks, work environment, educational requirements, average salaries, and job growth. In addition, the www.myfuture.com site supplements this information with additional details as you search each potential career.

Guided Questions

- Do you like to be hands on or work at a desk?
- Do you want to be creative in solving problems or be adept at applying current knowledge and techniques?
- Are you drawn to natural sciences, medical sciences, or technology?
- Do you prefer a profession that is heavy or light in math?
- Do you prefer a profession that is heavy or light in memorization?
- Do you like to travel or even move to new locations?
- Do you want a career that is employable anywhere you go?
- Do you want to live in a city or in a rural location?
- Are you open to working abroad?
- Do you want to be able to telecommute (work from home)?
- Do you thrive on or buckle under stress and deadlines?
- Do you want to make life/death decisions?
- Do you like to be the leader or the follower?
- Do you like to work alone or in teams?
- Do you like to work with strangers (like customers or patients)?
- Do you like to work with animals?
- Do you want to have a direct impact on people, animals, or the planet?

- Do you want to make non-essentials like toys, games, and gadgets?
- Do you like to learn?
- Do you like responsibility and ownership?
- Do you like to explore new ideas or make current ones more efficient?
- Do you like the bragging rights of a specific job title?
- Do you want to work for yourself or for a company?
- How important are salary and benefits?
- Do you want to get started ASAP, or can you go to school for a while?

After answering these questions, pick the ones that matter most to you and measure your prospective careers against those criteria. Be flexible, but be honest with yourself. The next few sections give you some additional guidelines on coming up with careers that align with your interests.

Impact

Many people want a career that makes a difference in the world in one way or another. You can choose careers that impact humanity; that help the environment, plants, and animals; or that add to our knowledge of the world. Within each category, you can decide if you want to work with the public and clients, with nature, or with things and ideas. In addition, you want to consider whether the output of your career addresses essential needs, creature comforts, or future innovations. Figure 8-1 shows a graphical organization of thoughts on career impact.

		Work Addresses		
Impact On	**Work With**	Essential Needs	Comforts	Future Innovations
People	People			
People	Nature			
People	Ideas/Things			
Nature	People			
Nature	Nature			
Nature	Ideas/Things			
Knowledge	People			
Knowledge	Nature			
Knowledge	Ideas/Things			

Figure 8-1: Organizing ideas around career impact.

If you want to have an impact on people, the majority of careers are aimed at just that. After all, people are the paying customers, so they are the ones that create the jobs. If you want to have an impact on humanity and like working with the public as in the top row of Figure 8-1, then a career in health sciences is an obvious choice. Within these fields, you can work on essential, life and death kinds of care as a nurse or a doctor. You can work to improve comfort, mobility, or quality of life like a physical or occupational therapist, optometrist, or dentist. You could also work in the field of mathematics and meet with clients to help them plan for the future (personal financial advisor) or to gain feedback for new products and services (market analyst). Professors also deal with the public to help students to a future career.

If you want to impact people, but are more comfortable working in the field or in a lab as in the second row of Figure 8-1, you may consider many of the natural sciences. Jobs that focus on essential needs are ones like epidemiologist, medical scientist, and biophysicist. Addressing issues of comfort and mobility can be done as a prosthetist or orthotist (people who design artificial limbs, for example). Helping people prepare for the future are specialties of the atmospheric scientist and agricultural scientist.

You can also impact people by working mainly with things and ideas (third row of Figure 8-1). For example, economists, statisticians, and geographers analyze things from global financial trends to health statistics to cultural impacts from various phenomena. Computer hardware and software developers can create automation for medical records and procedures, new gadgets that make our lives easier, or new means for improving human communications. Depending on the individual job or project, these professions can impact essentials, comforts, or future innovations.

If you want to impact the environment, plants, or animals, obvious choices would include conservationist, environmental scientist, marine biologist, zoologist, or veterinarian. Most of these jobs are in the field or lab environment (fifth row of Figure 8-1). Many also deal directly with the public as concerned clients or as a body of people that can provide funding or become more educated (fourth row). Jobs in these fields can give essential life and death care, provide better quality of life to an animal, or preserve an endangered habitat or resource.

Finally, if you want to impact the realm of ideas and knowledge, you will likely be working in the field or lab or modeling predictions on a computer as per the last two rows of Figure 8-1. Mathematicians, physicists, astronomers, and many engineers do just that.

Day to Day Experiences

Determining where and how you would like to impact the world will help narrow the field of choices to some extent. But, many people also care about what their job will be like on a day to day basis. For example, do you like to be hands on, or are you more comfortable at a desk? If you are choosing careers that work directly with people or natural phenomena, then you will likely be doing a lot of field or lab work. If you like working more with ideas and concepts, then computer work is more likely in your future.

Similarly, if your area of impact is people and environment, you will likely be working in the applied areas of science – using existing knowledge to create useful devices, procedures, or outcomes. If you are impacting the field of knowledge, your work will be more theoretical in nature. You may also consider that of the careers impacting people and nature, some are low stress, some are fast paced, and others involve life and death decision-making either with careful contemplation or with fraction of a second response times. It's important to realize what the job entails and whether you would thrive or fail in such environments.

In the natural science, engineering, and technical fields, you can also choose to work in research, development, or manufacturing. Research refers to coming up with new ideas and testing them for success whether your work has an applied or theoretical focus. It provides the most opportunities for patents and publications. Research usually has a more relaxed environment than development, and requires the most schooling.

Development takes the ideas from research and turns them into something a company can sell, either in large quantities (like consumer products) or small quantities (such as business or government goods). This involves improving on the ideas from the research department for usability and manufacturability. Opportunities for patents and publications can be plentiful. Work in this field is a bit faster-paced with more deadlines and demands. The work typically involves larger teams than those in research, and management opportunities can sometimes be a little better. The schooling requirement is still hefty, but sometimes not as high as that of the research requirements, depending on the field of study and the company.

Manufacturing takes the products from development and puts them into a production facility. People in these fields have diverse responsibilities including adapting manufacturing equipment, tweaking faults with the product, managing large teams of skilled or unskilled labor, ensuring safe and legal practices, and putting out the daily fires that threaten to derail budget and schedule. This is the most hectic and stressful of the three fields, but it can also be rewarding with its direct impact on the final product as well as the opportunity to be a hero on a daily basis. It typically requires less formal education.

Additional day to day considerations in any field include the types of hours you work. Many of the medical professions can require evening and weekend hours as well as being on call (available at a moment's notice to come into work). Manufacturing jobs are often like this, as well. Certain science professions may from time to time require more schedule flexibility to coincide with an optimum rocket launch window or a natural phenomenon. Most jobs tend to have regular hours, even those in medical professions where life and death impact is minimal. Still other jobs, those that mostly revolve around desk work, lend themselves well to telecommuting and working from home.

Other factors to consider involve where you might live and how much time you'll spend there. People in most medical fields can live anywhere there are people. Engineering and technical people tend to cluster near cities or developed areas. Some have opportunities to work abroad. Jobs that study the environment, plants, and animals may require a certain proximity to bodies of water, forests, mountains, or the like. A profession may require a lot of travel to conduct first hand inspections or to meet with prospective clients. Other jobs may require very little travel except for the occasional technical conferences or customer meetings.

You may also want to consider whether you want to own your own business, be an independent contractor, or work for someone else in private industry, non-profit organizations, schools, government, or the military. Most professions have opportunities in all of these venues depending on the level of education and your particular interests.

If you decide to work with other people, you should consider if you want to be a manager, a team player, or a sole contributor (a person who is self-paced, working mostly alone). Management opportunities usually come with experience, and the amount of team interaction will be dependent of the scope of the projects you take on. Obviously developing a web site is a smaller project than building a naval ship. Once in your chosen field, you may have other choices to make such as continuing to be a technical person or moving into people or project management.

Figure 8-2 summarizes the discussion of the day to day experience considerations when choosing a career.

Type of Work	Stress	Hours
Hands On or Desk	Low	Regular
Applied or Theoretical	High	Irregular or Flexible
R&D or Manufacturing	Life/Death	On-Call
Home Life	**Employer**	**Work Team**
Rural or Urban	Self-Employed	Sole Contributer
Live Abroad	Industry	Team Player
Travel	Government, School, Military	Manager

Figure 8-2: Day to day experience considerations.

Preparation

With the cost of schooling such as it is many people need to understand how many years they have to invest before they start making real money. There are a number of STEM jobs that pay over $55,000 in median annual salary and only require two years of schooling. Keep in mind that median salary means you will be earning a bit less when you are fresh out of school. In the medical fields, two year education requirements fit jobs such as radiation therapist, MRI technologist, registered nurse, and respiratory therapist. In the technical fields, there are web designers and IT specialists. And, in engineering, there are technicians in fields such as aerospace, electrical, mechanical, environmental, nuclear, and petroleum engineering with jobs available in development and manufacturing.

Jobs that require four years of education include most of the technical and engineering specialties. With a four year education in these fields, you may be working in a development or manufacturing environment or with the government. Exceptions exist, of course. There are also a number of natural and health science careers as well as math careers that only require a baccalaureate degree.

Obviously there are many jobs that require 2-4 years beyond college. Obtaining advanced degrees in some disciplines enable a broader opportunity for positions in research or as a professor.

Other considerations for preparation time include requirements outside of school. Many of the medical professions can require multiple years of internship or residency with varying levels of pay. Most, if not all, medical professions as well as other fields of study require licensure or certification predicated on passing a national exam or series of exams. Some exams additionally require a certain amount of industry experience before they can be taken.

In engineering disciplines that deal directly with the public or involve health, safety, and infrastructure, licensing and certification are required. In all engineering disciplines, licensing and certification are available if you wish to become a "professional engineer" who is eligible to give testimony in court hearings. Figure 8-3 gives a chart that can help you organize thoughts on preparation time.

		Certifications	No Certifications
Education	2 years		
	4 years		
	6 years		
	8 years		
Internship	1-2 years		
	3-5 years		
	6-10 years		
	Total Time:		

Figure 8-3: Organizing ideas around career preparation time.

As with any career choice, it is important to know what it will take to train you for an actual job. That is the point of going to college in the first place. Keep in mind that if you opt for a two year program in order to start earning money sooner, you still have the opportunity to go back to school and earn additional degrees, if you want to do so. You may get an employer to foot the bill in return for a certain number of years promised to the company. This may entail going to night school while working full-time, splitting time between work and school, or even returning to school full-time.

If you opt for a four year program, it's even more likely that employers may be willing to send you back to school. You may opt for additional technical degrees or for a Master's of Business Administration (M.B.A.). If you think you would be interested in returning to school, mention it in your job interview to see if such opportunities exist.

Should you decide to go further than four years on your own, you will find that many of the STEM disciplines outside of the medical fields will have opportunities for free graduate school and even part-time work. Within the medical fields, the Stafford loan limits for graduate programs are fairly high.

If you find yourself second-guessing how much education is required to do what you want, I encourage you to seek out professors in your major or other professionals working similar jobs. Reaching out through social media, reading online articles, and asking friends of friends are ways to gather more specific information about the highs and lows of any career.

Final Comments

In the end, you are the one who should decide what is right for you. STEM careers offer many benefits that will help you stay on top of the sinking middle class or even launch you into the upper echelons. But, STEM careers also require a high entrance fee of hard work, dedication, and the ability to pay for college no matter how long it takes. That's why there's no fear of "glutting the market:" producing more STEM graduates than there are jobs to support. If you feel strongly that you have another calling, I wish you Godspeed. But, just be sure that no one subject, no one financial roadblock, no one dissenting comment, no one bad teacher, no one bigot or chauvinist – NO ONE – is making that decision for you.

No matter where your ship is headed, I wish you great success!

Index

A

abstraction	54
achievement gap	18
advisor	83
affirmative action	118
affordable care act	13
age income gap	5
AMCAS	82
anticipating next thing	55
autonomy	77

B

B.S. degree by ethnicity	107
B.S. degree by gender	89
B.S. in STEM by ethnicity	108
B.S. in STEM by gender	90
benefits	28
bonus	28
bookkeeping	50
building confidence	51
business professions	39

C

career impact	126
career questions	125
certifications	133
child care	87
chilly climate	101
choosing a college	76
civilian options for college	65
class mobility	5,13
college costs	62
college v. family income	18
committee	83
community college	68
compensation	27
consumer price index (CPI)	10
cooperative education	68,76,86
cost of graduate school	37
cost of living	69
culture conflict	97,114

Index

D-E

day to day career experiences	129
defense	83
deferment period	65
dependent status	66
development	129
discrimination by ethnicity	117
discrimination by gender	100
dissertation	83
double bind	91,117
employer paid degrees	29,69,134
engineering careers	35
estimating reasonable tuition	70
executive order on education	120

F-G

factory jobs	14
FAFSA	65
fears about STEM	39
finding hidden patterns	53
free graduate school	37,134
GI Bill	64
glutting the market	32
grading on a curve	78
graduate assistantship	84
graduate workload	86
GRE	83
groundwork for grad school	85

H-I

health care costs	13
health sciences careers	33
high poverty schools	116
Hispanic outreach programs	120
historic change in income	7,8
historic costs of college	17
historic CPI	10
historic federal minimum wage	11
historic share of income	7
historic SS COLA	12
impact	33
income distribution by job	94
income inequality	7
independent status	66
infrastructure jobs	14
in-state status	68
insurance plans	29
interest in STEM, by ethnicity	110
interest in STEM, by gender	93
internship	82,133

J-L

job placement	61
job sharing	87
law professions	38
lay-off protection	32
licensing	133

loan limits, graduate & medical	67		
licensing	131	**N-O**	
loan limits, undergraduate	66	NAEP math test by ethnicity	113
loan repayment	69	NAEP math test by gender	96
logic	47	NAEP science test by ethnicity	113
long term disability	29	NAEP science test by gender	97
low poverty schools	116	natural, phys. sciences careers	34
		need-based aid	65
M		need for math	56
		new perspectives	54
management style	87	non-medical career v. education	84
managerial positions	39	non-thesis option	83
manufacturing	130	NOW 2 kNOW Math Series	57
Master's Degree	83		
math in STEM	45	on-campus v. off-campus	61
mathematics careers	35	organizing details	49
mean income v. education	15	out-of-state status	68
mean net worth v. education	15		
mean salary by occupation	38	**P-Q**	
median earnings v. 4 yr degree	37		
median earnings v. education	14	paid time off	29
median income by ethnicity	115	patience	52
median net worth by ethnicity	115	pattern seeking	52
medical career v. education	82	PayScale survey	27
medical school	81	Pell Grants	16
military options for college	63	personal loans	67
miscellaneous college costs	63	Ph.D.	83
misconceptions about STEM	39	Ph.D. in STEM by ethnicity	108
mismatch	118	PLUS loan	67
		poverty	114
		preparation time for careers	132

professional engineer	133
professions of the top 1%	19
qualifier exam	84

R

rational thinking	48
relocation expenses	29
research	129
research assistantship	84
residency	82, 133
retirement plan, 401k	28
return on investment	16
room and board	61
ROTC	64

S

SATM scores by ethnicity	112
SATM scores by gender	96
scholarships	65
school size	75
seeing the big picture	49
selected careers v. ethnicity	109
selected careers v. gender	91
short term disability	29
shortage of STEM graduates	30
social equality	18
social security benefit	12
spatial reasoning	55, 98
spotting similarities	52
standard of living	10
stereotype threat	99, 114
stipend	84
stock option	28
subsidized Stafford loan	65
surviving undergrad	80

T

teaching assistantship	84
technology careers	34
telecommuting	87, 130
thesis option	83
top 10 2013 annual salaries	28
top 10 salaries by 4 yr degree	27
tracking details	50
travel opportunities	29
trickle down economics	7
tuition and fees	61

U-Z

U.S. population by ethnicity	107
U.S. population by gender	89
undergraduate workload	77
unemployment rate v. educ.	14
unemployment rate v. occup.	31
unsubsidized Stafford loan	65
using tools creatively	53
wealth distribution, 2010	9
wealth inequality	7
women in STEM	87
women of color in STEM	92

The NOW 2 kNOW™ Math Series

The NOW 2 kNOW™ Mathematics Philosophy

If you are struggling with math, you don't have time to read a 400 page "help" book. You need the main concepts laid out simply yet thoroughly.

The NOW 2 kNOW™ math texts give complete instruction in *80 pages or less*! In addition, you'll find *over 200* problems with *worked out* solutions!

See why math doesn't have to be hard or time-consuming to learn!

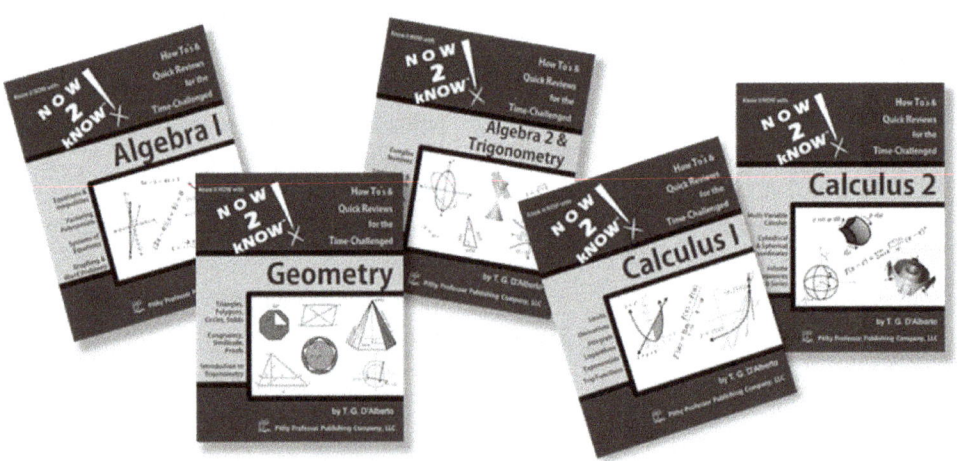

NOW 2 kNOW™
High Paying Careers in STEM, 2nd Ed.

- Over 80 careers with >$55,000 median salary
- Job Description
- Daily Tasks
- Work Environment
- Education Requirements
- Median Pay
- Job Growth

Available on Amazon.com or NOW2kNOW.com

www.ingramcontent.com/pod-product-compliance
Lightning Source LLC
Chambersburg PA
CBHW080512110426
42742CB00017B/3091